Contents

Index of Authors   viii

Preface   ix

Man and Beast
Caring for Animals   *Jon Silkin*   2
Wilderness   *Carl Sandburg*   3
The Tyger   *William Blake*   4
The King   *Douglas Livingstone*   5
Cat   *Alan Brownjohn*   6
The Early Purges   *Seamus Heaney*   7
The Secret in the Cat   *May Swenson*   8
Dissection   *Colin Rowbotham*   9
The Rabbit   *Alan Brownjohn*   10
The Meadow Mouse   *Theodore Roethke*   12
Death of a Bird   *Jon Silkin*   13
If the Owl Calls Again   *John Haines*   14
Owl   *George Macbeth*   15
Parrot   *Alan Brownjohn*   17
A Robin   *Walter de la Mare*   17
The Best Beast of the Fat-Stock Show at Earl's Court   *Stevie Smith*   18
The Arrival of the Bee Box   *Sylvia Plath*   20
The Disclosure   *Denise Levertov*   21
To the Snake   *Denise Levertov*   22
Snake   *Emily Dickinson*   22
The Lizard   *Theodore Roethke*   23
Workshop   24

You
Metaphors   *Sylvia Plath*   26
Morning Song   *Sylvia Plath*   26
Baby's Drinking Song   *James Kirkup*   27
A Child Half-Asleep   *Tony Connor*   28
Children's Song   *R S Thomas*   28
Warning to Children   *Robert Graves*   29
To My Daughter   *Stephen Spender*   30
At Seven a Son   *Elaine Feinstein*   30
My Parents Kept Me   *Stephen Spender*   31
How to Catch Tiddlers   *Brian Jones*   32
Death of a Naturalist   *Seamus Heaney*   33
The Rag Doll to the Heedless Child   *David Harsent*   34
Death of God   *Graham Walley*   34
Micky Thumps   *Anon*   35
Who Do You Think You Are?   *Carl Sandburg*   36
Thoughts   *Michael Benedikt*   37

Hodder & Stoughton
LONDON SYDNEY AUCKLAND

PoetryWorkshop

Michael &
Peter Benton

The Cauliflower   *John Haines*   38
Fledglings   *William Meredith*   38
Dream of the Cardboard Lover   *John Haines*   39
Dream Variation   *Langston Hughes*   39
First Ice   *Andrey Voznesensky*   40
Idyll   *traditional African*   41
Love Poem   *Douglas Dunn*   41
Fifteen Line Sonnet in Four Parts   *Stephen Spender*   41
Visiting Miss Emily   *Brian Jones*   42
Crabbed Age and Youth   *William Shakespeare*   43
The Old Couple   *F Pratt Green*   44
Old People   *D H Lawrence*   45
Workshop   46

The World Around You

Winter   *Walter de la Mare*   49
Winter Moon   *Jeremy Hooker*   49
And When the Green Man Comes   *John Haines*   50
Thaw   *Brian Jones*   50
In Nature   *John Haines*   50
Clouds   *G M Hopkins*   51
Summer Waterfall, Glendale   *Norman MacCaig*   52
Weather Bestiary   *George Mackay Brown*   52
A Haiku Yearbook   *Anthony Thwaite*   53
Sunday Morning   *Wes Magee*   54
Moorings   *Norman MacCaig*   54
At the Fishhouses   *Elizabeth Bishop*   56
To the Sea   *Philip Larkin*   58
The Bonfire   *Anthony Thwaite*   59
A Heap of Stones   *Richard Ryan*   60
The Hippopotamusman   *Roger McGough*   62
I Return to the Place I Was Born   *T'Ao Yuan Ming*   63
On Roofs of Terry Street   *Douglas Dunn*   63
The Place's Fault   *Philip Hobsbaum*   64
From the Night-Window   *Douglas Dunn*   65
Hotel Room, 12th Floor   *Norman MacCaig*   66
Ballad of the Landlord   *Langston Hughes*   67
Workshop   68

Five Poets

Ted Hughes   70   The Warm and the Cold   72
                           The Jaguar   73
                           Snowdrop   73
                           Examination at the Womb Door   74
                           Crow's Song of Himself   75
                           King of Carrion   75

Sylvia Plath 76   Mushrooms 76
You're 77
A Winter Ship 79
Balloons 80

Seamus Heaney 81   Blackberry-Picking 81
Digging 82
The Barn 83
The Forge 83
Limbo 84

Robert Frost 86   Design 86
The Road Not Taken 86
The Runaway 87
Lodged 87
Nothing Gold Can Stay 87
At Woodward's Gardens 88
'Out, Out–' 89
Spring Pools 90

Brian Patten 91   Little Johnny's Confession 91
Little Johnny's Final Letter 92
The Projectionist's Nightmare 92
Mr Jones Takes Over 92
Bombscare 93
A Small Dragon 93

Workshop 94

Children's Rhymes

Sam, Sam the dirty man 96
Oh my finger 96
Ladies and Gentlemen 96
Isn't it funny 96
Down in the Valley 96
An Egg 97
A Lighted Candle 97
I wet my finger 97
Same to you 97
Touch Collar 97
A Duck in a Pond 97
While Shepherds Watched 97
We Three Kings 97
Mary Had 97
In 1492 97
Splishy Splashy 97
Sir is kind 97
No more Latin 97

Poems and Pictures

Autumn Grove After Rain, by Wen Tien   *James Kirkup*   99
Landscape, by Ch'êng Sui   *James Kirkup*   99
The Artist, Arles 1890   *Colin Rowbotham*   100
Van Gogh, Cornfield with Crows   *James O Taylor*   101
In Breughel's Panorama   *Sylvia Plath*   102

Workshop   103

Reflections
Mirror   *Sylvia Plath*   104
A Strange Old Man   *Hitomaro*   104
Withered Reeds   *Ranko*   106
The Door Knob   *Robin Skelton*   108
Workshop   109

Shapes
Watchwords   *Roger McGough*   110
Archives   *Edwin Morgan*   111
The Fan   *Malcolm Timperley*   112
Easter Wings   *George Herbert*   112
The Crosse-Tree   *Robert Herrick*   113
Revolver   *Alan Riddell*   114
Upon His Departure Hence   *Robert Herrick*   116
here's a little mouse)and   *e. e. cummings*   116
Heart and Mirror   *Guillaume Apollinaire*   116
Workshop   117

Songs
Little Boxes   *M Reynolds*   118
Lucy in the Sky with Diamonds   *Lennon & McCartney*   119
She's Leaving Home   *Lennon & McCartney*   120
When I'm 64   *Lennon & McCartney*   121
Road Builders   *Anon*   122
The Driver's Song   *Ewan MacColl*   122
Come, me Little Son   *Ewan MacColl*   123
The Fitter's Song   *Ewan MacColl*   124
Bridge over Troubled Water   *P Simon*   125
Workshop   126

Looking and Seeing
Observation   *W Hart-Smith*   127
Dandelion   *Jon Silkin*   128
Snowdrop   *Jon Silkin*   128
Meditation at Oyster River   *Theodore Roethke*   129
Relic   *Ted Hughes*   130
Perfect   *Hugh MacDiarmid, Glyn Jones*   130
The Chalk Blue Butterfly   *Stephen Spender*   131
Workshop   132

Masks
Poem to be Cast in Bronze   *Robin Skelton*   134
The Mask of Evil   *Bertolt Brecht*   134
Workshop   135

Acknowledgments   136

Index of authors

Anon   35, 122
Apollinaire, Guillaume   116

Benedikt, Michael   37
Bishop, Elizabeth   56
Brecht, Bertolt   134
Brownjohn, Alan   6, 10, 17

Connor, Tony   28
cummings, e. e.   116

De La Mare, Walter   17, 49
Dickinson, Emily   22
Dunn, Douglas   41, 63, 65

Feinstein, Elaine   30
Frost, Robert   86–90

Graves, Robert   29

Haines, John   14, 39, 50
Harsent, David   34
Hart-Smith, W   127
Heaney, Seamus   7, 33, 81–4
Herbert, George   112
Herrick, Robert   113, 116
Hitomaro   104
Hobsbaum, Philip   64
Hooker, Jeremy   49
Hopkins, G M   51
Hughes, Langston   39, 67
Hughes, Ted   70–75, 130

Jones, Brian   32, 42, 50

Kirkup, James   27, 98, 99

Larkin, Philip   58
Lawrence, D H   45
Lennon, John   119–21
Levertov, Denise   21, 22
Livingstone, Douglas   5

Macbeth, George   15
MacCaig, Norman   52, 54, 66
MacColl, Ewan   122–4
MacDiarmid, Hugh   130
McCartney, Paul   119–21
McGough, Roger   62, 110
MacKay Brown, George   52
Magee, Wes   54
Meredith, William   38
Morgan, Edwin   111

Patten, Brian   91–3
Plath, Sylvia   20, 26, 76–80, 102, 104
Pratt Green, F   44

Ranko   106
Reynolds, M   118
Riddell, Alan   114
Roethke, Theodore   12, 23, 129
Rowbotham, Colin   9, 100
Ryan, Richard   60

Sandburg, Carl   3, 36
Shakespeare, William   43
Silkin, Jon   2, 13, 128
Simon, P   125
Skelton, Robin   108, 134
Smith, Stevie   18
Spender, Stephen   30, 31, 41, 131
Swenson, May   8

T'Ao, Yuan Ming   63
Taylor, James O   101
Thomas, R S   28
Thwaite, Anthony   53, 59
Timperley, Malcolm   112
Traditional   41, 96, 97

Voznesensky, Andrey   40

Walley, Graham   34

Preface

Poetry Workshop is a source book of ideas and materials for work in English with pupils between the ages of thirteen and sixteen. In compiling this anthology of poems and pictures we have in mind the interests and needs of children in the two or three years leading up to their public examinations at CSE or GCE, and we hope that teachers will find here both a flexible and imaginative approach which still makes considerable literary and creative demands upon their pupils.

The book is, deliberately, 'activities based', opening up through its eleven workshops a widely varied English programme of discussion, drama, projects, creative and critical writing, the aim of which is to suggest starting points for activities which we hope will be both enjoyable and offer something to pupils over a wide range of abilities. Accordingly, most of the workshops invite children to talk in small groups, and often encourage informal discussion and individual choice. As all invitations, it can be politely declined, but we hope that teachers using this book will exploit at least some of the opportunities for variety in teaching methods which we suggest in the workshops, although limited space and a desire not to presume to dictate lessons mean that these sections are fairly short and *must* be expanded and modified according to the individual classroom situation. We are well aware that by encouraging a more flexible approach to English we are also encouraging more organisational problems for the teacher. At the risk of being too prescriptive, therefore, we have often given specific details of how classes or groups might be arranged, in the belief that the vast majority of pupils need a firm framework before they can explore their own freedom of choice most profitably.

M G B

P B

Poetry
Workshop

MAN & BEAST

Caring for Animals

I ask sometimes why these small animals
With bitter eyes, why we should care for them.

I question the sky, the serene blue water,
But it cannot say. It gives no answer.

And no answer releases in my head
A procession of grey shades patched and whimpering,

Dogs with clipped ears, wheezing cart horses
A fly without shadow and without thought.

Is it with these menaces to our vision
With this procession led by a man carrying wood

We must be concerned? The holy land, the rearing
Green island should be kindlier than this.

Yet the animals, our ghosts, need tending to.
Take in the whipped cat and the blinded owl;

Take up the man-trapped squirrel upon your shoulder.
Attend to the unnecessary beasts.

From growing mercy and a moderate love
Great love for the human animal occurs.

And your love grows. Your great love grows and grows.

JON SILKIN

Wilderness

There is a wolf in me ... fangs pointed for tearing gashes ...
a red tongue for raw meat ... and the hot lapping of
blood – I keep this wolf because the wilderness gave it to
me and the wilderness will not let it go.

There is a fox in me ... a silver-gray fox ... I sniff and
guess ... I pick things out of the wind and air ... I nose in
the dark night and take sleepers and eat them and hide the
feathers ... I circle and loop and double-cross.

There is a hog in me ... a snout and a belly ... a machinery
for eating and grunting ... a machinery for sleeping
satisfied in the sun – I got this too from the wilderness and
the wilderness will not let it go.

There is a fish in me ... I know I came from salt-blue
water-gates ... I scurried with shoals of herring ... I blew
waterspouts with porpoises ... before land was ... before
the water went down ... before Noah ... before the first
chapter of Genesis.

There is a baboon in me ... clambering-clawed ...
dog-faced ... yawping a galoot's* hunger ... hairy under   *rough lout
the armpits ... here are the hawk-eyed hankering men ...
here are the blond and blue-eyed women ... here they
hide curled asleep waiting ... ready to snarl and kill ...
ready to sing and give milk ... waiting – I keep the
baboon because the wilderness says so.

There is an eagle in me and a mockingbird ... and the eagle
flies among the Rocky Mountains of my dreams and
fights among the Sierra crags of what I want ... and the
mockingbird warbles in the early forenoon before the dew
is gone, warbles in the underbrush of my Chattanoogas
of hope, gushes over the blue Ozark foothills of my
wishes – And I got the eagle and the mockingbird from the
wilderness.

O, I got a zoo, I got a menagerie, inside my ribs, under my
bony head, under my red-valve heart – and I got something
else: it is a man-child heart, a woman-child heart: it is a
father and mother and lover: it came from God-Knows-
Where: it is going to God-Knows-Where – For I am the
keeper of the zoo: I say yes and no: I sing and kill and
work: I am a pal of the world. I came from the wilderness.

CARL SANDBURG

3

The Tyger

Tyger Tyger, burning bright,
In the forests of the night;
What immortal hand or eye,
Could frame thy fearful symmetry?

In what distant deeps or skies
Burnt the fire of thine eyes!
On what wings dare he aspire!
What the hand, dare seize the fire?

And what shoulder, & what art,
Could twist the sinews of thy heart?
And when thy heart began to beat,
What dread hand? & what dread feet?

What the hammer? what the chain,
In what furnace was thy brain?
What the anvil? what dread grasp,
Dare its deadly terrors clasp!

When the stars threw down their spears
And water'd heaven with their tears:
Did he smile his work to see?
Did he who made the Lamb make thee?

Tyger Tyger burning bright,
In the forests of the night;
What immortal hand or eye,
Dare frame thy fearful symmetry?

The King

Old Tawny's mane is moth-
eaten now, a balding monk's tonsure
and his fluid thigh muscles flop
slack as an exhausted boxer's;

Creaks a little and is
just a fraction under fast (he's lame)
in those last short lethal rushes
at the slim white-eyed winging game;

Can catch them still of course,
the horny old claws combing crimson
from the velvet flanks in long scores,
here in the game-park's environs;

Each year, panting heavily,
manages with aged urbanity
to smile full-faced and yellowly
at a thousand box cameras.

Douglas Livingstone

5

Cat

Sometimes I am an unseen
marmalade cat, the friendliest colour,
making off through a window without permission,
pacing along a broken-glass wall to the
    greenhouse,
jumping down with a soft, four-pawed thump,
finding two inches open of the creaking door
with the loose brass handle,
slipping impossibly in,
flattening my fur at the hush and touch of
    the sudden warm air,
avoiding the tiled gutter of slow green water,
skirting the potted nests of tetchy cactuses,
and sitting with my tail flicked
skilfully underneath me, to sniff
the azaleas   the azaleas   the azaleas.

ALAN BROWNJOHN

The Early Purges

I was six when I first saw kittens drown.
Dan Taggart pitched them, 'the scraggy wee shits',
Into a bucket; a frail metal sound,

Soft paws scraping like mad. But their tiny din
Was soon soused. They were slung on the snout
Of the pump and the water pumped in.

'Sure isn't it better for them now?' Dan said.
Like wet gloves they bobbed and shone till he sluiced
Them out on the dunghill, glossy and dead.

Suddenly frightened, for days I sadly hung
Round the yard, watching the three sogged remains
Turn mealy and crisp as old summer dung

Until I forgot them. But the fear came back
When Dan trapped big rats, snared rabbits, shot crows
Or, with a sickening tug, pulled old hens' necks.

Still, living displaces false sentiments
And now, when shrill pups are prodded to drown
I just shrug, 'Bloody pups'. It makes sense:

'Prevention of cruelty' talk cuts ice in town
Where they consider death unnatural,
But on well-run farms pests have to be kept down.

SEAMUS HEANEY

7

The Secret in the Cat

I took my cat apart
to see what made him purr.
Like an electric clock
or like the snore

of a warming kettle,
something fizzled and sizzled in him.
Was he a soft car,
the engine bubbling sound?

Was there a wire beneath his fur,
or humming throttle?
I undid his throat.
Within was no stir.

I opened up his chest
as though it were a door:
no whisk or rattle there.
I lifted off his skull:

no hiss or murmur.
I halved his little belly
but found no gear,
no cause for static.

So I replaced his lid,
laced his little gut.
His heart into his vest I slid
and buttoned up his throat.

His tail rose to a rod
and beckoned to the air.
Some voltage made him vibrate
warmer than before.

Whiskers and a tail:
perhaps they caught
some radar code
emitted as a pip, a dot-and-dash

of woollen sound.
My cat a kind of tuning fork? —
amplifier? — telegraph? —
doing secret signal work?

His eyes elliptic tubes:
there's a message in his stare.
I stroke him
but cannot find the dial.   [MAY SWENSON

Dissection This rat looks like it is made of marzipan
Soft and neatly packaged in its envelope;
I shake it free.
Fingering the damp, yellow fur, I know
That this first touch is far the worst.

    There is a book about it that contains
Everything on a rat, with diagrams
Meticulous, but free from blood
Or all the yellow juices
I will have to pour away.

    Now peg it out:
My pins are twisted and the board is hard
But, using force and fracturing its legs
I manage though
And crucify my rat.

    From the crutch to the throat the fur is ripped
Not neatly, not as shown in the diagrams,
But raggedly;
My hacking has revealed the body wall
As a sack that is fat with innards to be torn
By the inquisitive eye
And the hand that strips aside.

    Inside this taut, elastic sack is a surprise;
Not the chaos I had thought to find,
No oozing mash; instead of that
A firmly coiled discipline
Of overlapping liver, folded gut;
A neatness that is like a small machine –
And I wonder what it is that has left this rat,
Why a month of probing could not make it go again,
What it is that has disappeared…

    The bell has gone; it is time to go for lunch.
I fold the rat, replace it in its bag,
Wash from my hands the sweet
Smell of meat and formalin
And go and eat a meat pie afterwards.

    So, for four weeks or so, I am told
I shall continue to dissect this rat;
Like a child
Pulling apart a clock he cannot mend.   [COLIN ROWBOTHAM

The Rabbit

(After Prévert)

We are going to see the rabbit.
We are going to see the rabbit.
Which rabbit, people say?
Which rabbit, ask the children?
Which rabbit?
The only rabbit.
The only rabbit in England,
Sitting behind a barbed-wire fence
Under the floodlights, neon lights,
Sodium lights,
Nibbling grass
On the only patch of grass
In England, in England
(Except the grass by the hoardings
Which doesn't count.)
We are going to see the rabbit.
And we must be there on time.

First we shall go by escalator,
Then we shall go by underground,
And then we shall go by motorway
And then by helicopterway,
And the last ten yards we shall have to go
On foot.

And now we are going
All the way to see the rabbit,
We are nearly there,
We are longing to see it,
And so is the crowd
Which is here in thousands
With mounted policemen
And big loudspeakers
And bands and banners,
And everyone has come a long way.
But soon we shall see it
Sitting and nibbling
The blades of grass
On the only patch of grass
In – but something has gone wrong!
Why is everyone so angry,
Why is everyone jostling
And slanging and complaining?

The rabbit has gone,
Yes, the rabbit has gone.
He has actually burrowed down into the earth,
And made himself a warren, under the earth,
Despite all these people.
And what shall we do?
What *can* we do?

It is all a pity, you must be disappointed,
Go home and do something else for today,
Go home again, go home for today.
For you cannot hear the rabbit, under the earth,
Remarking rather sadly to himself, by himself,
As he rests in his warren, under the earth;
'It won't be long, they are bound to come,
They are bound to come and find me, even here.'

ALAN BROWNJOHN

The Meadow Mouse

I

In a shoe box stuffed in an old nylon stocking
Sleeps the baby mouse I found in the meadow,
Where he trembled and shook beneath a stick
Till I caught him up by the tail and brought him in,
Cradled in my hand,
A little quaker, the whole body of him trembling,
His absurd whiskers sticking out like a cartoon-mouse,
His feet like small leaves,
Little lizard-feet,
Whitish and spread wide when he tried to struggle away,
Wriggling like a miniscule puppy.

Now he's eaten his three kinds of cheese and drunk from his
                                bottle-cap watering-trough –
So much he just lies in one corner,
His tail curled under him, his belly big
As his head; his bat-like ears
Twitching, tilting toward the least sound.

Do I imagine he no longer trembles
When I come close to him?
He seems no longer to tremble.

II

But this morning the shoe-box house on the back porch is empty.
Where has he gone, my meadow mouse,
My thumb of a child that nuzzled in my palm? –
To run under the hawk's wing,
Under the eye of the great owl watching from the elm-tree,
To live by courtesy of the shrike, the snake, the tom-cat.

I think of the nestling fallen into the deep grass,
The turtle gasping in the dusty rubble of the highway,
The paralytic stunned in the tub, and the water rising, –
All things innocent, hapless, forsaken.

THEODORE ROETHKE

Death of a Bird

After those first days
When we had placed him in his iron cage
  And made a space for him
    From such

Outrageous cage of wire,
Long and shallow, where the sunlight fell
  Through the air, onto him;
    After

He had been fed for three days
Suddenly, in that sunlight before noon
  He was dead with no
    Pretence.

He did not say goodbye
He did not say thankyou, but he died then
  Lying flat on the rigid
    Wires

Of his cage, his gold
Beak shut tight, which once in hunger had
  Opened as a trap
    And then

Swiftly closed again,
Swallowing quickly what I had given him;
  How can I say I am sorry
    He died.

Seeing him lie there dead,
Death's friend with death, I was angry he
  Had gone without pretext or warning,
    With no

Suggestion first he should go,
Since I had fed him, then put wires round him
  Bade him hop across
    The bars of my hands.

I asked him only that
He should desire his life. He had become
  Of us a black friend with
    A gold mouth

Shrilly singing through
The heat. The labour of the black bird! I
  Cannot understand why
    He is dead.

I bury him familiarly.
His heritage is a small brown garden.
Something is added to the everlasting earth;
From my mind a space is taken away.

JON SILKIN

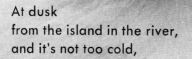

At dusk
from the island in the river,
and it's not too cold,

I'll wait for the moon
to rise,
then take wing and glide
to meet him.

We will not speak,
but hooded against the frost
soar above
the alder flats, searching
with tawny eyes.

And then we'll sit
in the shadowy spruce and
pick the bones
of careless mice,

while the long moon drifts
towards Asia
and the river mutters
in its icy bed.

And when morning climbs
the limbs
we'll part without a sound,
fulfilled, floating
homewards as
the cold world awakens.

JOHN HAINES

If the Owl Calls Again

Owl is my favourite. Who flies
like a nothing through the night,
who-whoing. Is a feather
duster in leafy corners ring-a-rosy-ing
boles of mice. Twice

you hear him call. Who
is he looking for? You hear
him hoovering over the floor
of the wood. O would you be gold
rings in the driving skull

if you could? Hooded and
vulnerable by the winter suns
owl looks. Is the grain of bark
in the dark. Round beaks are at
work in the pellety nest,

resting. Owl is an eye
in the barn. For a hole
in the trunk owl's blood
is to blame. Black talons in the
petrified fur! Cold walnut hands

on the case of the brain! In the reign
of the chicken owl comes like
a god. Is a goad in
the rain to the pink eyes,
dripping. For a meal in the day

flew, killed, on the moor. Six
mouths are the seed of his
arc in the season. Torn meat
from the sky. Owl lives
by the claws of his brain. On the branch

in the sever of the hand's
twigs owl is a backward look.
Flown wind in the skin. Fine
rain in the bones. Owl breaks
like the day. Am an owl, am an owl.

GEORGE MACBETH

Someone, perhaps a child, who is fascinated
by owls creates a sort of spell to bring an
owl into being. By the end of the poem he
has become the owl.   G.M.

Parrot

Sometimes I sit with both eyes closed,
But all the same, I've heard!
They're saying, 'He won't talk because
He is a *thinking* bird.'

I'm olive-green and sulky, and
The family say, 'Oh yes,
He's silent, but he's *listening*,
He *thinks* more than he *says*!

'He ponders on the things he hears,
Preferring not to chatter.'
– And this is true, but *why* it's true
Is quite another matter.

I'm working out some shocking things
In order to surprise them,
And when my thoughts are ready I'll
Certainly *not* disguise them!

I'll wait, and see, and choose a time
When everyone is present,
And clear my throat and raise my beak
And give a squawk and start to speak
And go on for about a week
And it will not be pleasant!

ALAN BROWNJOHN

A Robin

Ghost-grey the fall of night,
  Ice-bound the lane,
Lone in the dying light
  Flits he again;
Lurking where shadows steal,
Perched in his coat of blood,
Man's homestead at his heel,
  Death-still the wood.

Odd restless child; it's dark;
  All wings are flown
But this one wizard's – hark! –
  Stone clapped on stone!
Changeling and solitary,
Secret and sharp and small,
Flits he from tree to tree,
  Calling on all.

WALTER DE LA MARE

The Best Beast of The Fat-Stock Show at Earl's Court

(In monosyllables)

The Best Beast of the Show
Is fat,
He goes by the lift –
They all do that.

This lift, large as a room,
(Yet the beasts bunch),
Goes up with a groan,
They have not oiled the winch.

Not yet to the lift
Goes the Best Beast,
He has to walk on the floor to make a show
First.

Great are his horns,
Long his fur,
The Beast came from the North
To walk here.

Is he not fat?
Is he not fit?
Now in a crown he walks
To the lift.

When he lay in his pen,
In the close heat,
His head lolled, his eyes
Were not shut for sleep.

Slam the lift door,
Push it up with a groan,
Will they kill the Beast now?
Where has he gone?

When he lay in the straw
His heart beat so fast
His sides heaved, I touched his side
As I walked past.

I touched his side,
I touched the root of his horns;
The breath of the Beast
Came in low moans.

STEVIE SMITH

The Arrival of the Bee Box

I ordered this, this clean wood box
Square as a chair and almost too heavy to lift.
I would say it was the coffin of a midget
Or a square baby
Were there not such a din in it.

The box is locked, it is dangerous.
I have to live with it overnight
And I can't keep away from it.
There are no windows, so I can't see what is in there.
There is only a little grid, no exit.

I put my eye to the grid.
It is dark, dark,
With the swarmy feeling of African hands
Minute and shrunk for export,
Black on black, angrily clambering.

How can I let them out?
It is the noise that appals me most of all,
The unintelligible syllables.
It is like a Roman mob,
Small, taken one by one, but my god, together!

I lay my ear to furious Latin.
I am not a Caesar.
I have simply ordered a box of maniacs.
They can be sent back.
They can die, I need feed them nothing, I am the owner.

I wonder how hungry they are.
I wonder if they would forget me
If I just undid the locks and stood back and turned into a tree.
There is the laburnum, its blond colonnades,
And the petticoats of the cherry.

They might ignore me immediately
In my moon suit and funeral veil.
I am no source of honey
So why should they turn on me?
Tomorrow I will be sweet God, I will set them free.

The box is only temporary.

SYLVIA PLATH

20

The Disclosure

From the shrivelling gray
silk of its cocoon
a creature slowly
    is pushing out
to stand clear –

        not a butterfly,
            petal that floats at will across
            the summer breeze
        not a furred
        moth of the night
            crusted with indecipherable
            gold –

some primal-shaped, plain-winged, day-flying thing.

DENISE LEVERTOV

To the Snake

Green Snake, when I hung you round my neck
and stroked your cold, pulsing throat
    as you hissed to me, glinting
arrowy gold scales, and I felt
    the weight of you on my shoulders,
and the whispering silver of your dryness
    sounded close at my ears –

Green Snake – I swore to my companions that certainly
    you were harmless! But truly
I had no certainty, and no hope, only desiring
    to hold you, for that joy,
                which left
a long wake of pleasure, as the leaves moved
and you faded into the pattern
of grass and shadows, and I returned
smiling and haunted, to a dark morning.

DENISE LEVERTOV

Snake

A narrow Fellow in the Grass
Occasionally rides –
You may have met Him – did you not
His notice sudden is –

The Grass divides as with a Comb –
A spotted shaft is seen –
And then it closes at your feet
And opens further on –

He likes a Boggy Acre
A Floor too cool for Corn –
Yet when a Boy, and Barefoot –
I more than once at Noon
Have passed, I thought, a Whip lash
Unbraiding in the Sun –
When stooping to secure it
It wrinkled, and was gone –

Several of Nature's People
I know, and they know me –
I feel for them a transport
Of cordiality –

But never met this Fellow
Attended, or alone
Without a tighter breathing
And Zero at the Bone –

EMILY DICKINSON

The Lizard

He too has eaten well –
I can see that by the distended pulsing middle;
And his world and mine are the same,
The Mediterranean sun shining on us, equally,
His head, stiff as a scarab, turned to one side,
His right eye staring straight at me,
One leaf-like foot hung laxly
Over the worn curb of the terrace,
The tail straight as an awl,
Then suddenly flung up and over,
Ending curled around and over again,
A thread-like firmness.

(Would a cigarette disturb him?)

At the first scratch of the match
He turns his head slightly,
Retiring to nudge his neck half-way under
A dried strawberry leaf,
His tail gray with the ground now,
One round eye still toward me.
A white cabbage-butterfly drifts in,
Bumbling up and around the bamboo windbreak;
But the eye of the tiny lizard stays with me.
One greenish lid lifts a bit higher,
Then slides down over the eye's surface,
Rising again, slowly,
Opening, closing.

To whom does this terrace belong? –
With its limestone crumbling into fine grayish dust,
Its bevy of bees, and its wind-beaten rickety sun-chairs.
Not to me, but this lizard,
Older than I, or the cockroach.

THEODORE ROETHKE

Talking Points

What creatures have you kept as pets? What animals would you most like to keep? Why do people keep pets? ('Caring for Animals' p. 2)

Should we keep animals in captivity? Do you approve or disapprove of circuses …? hunting …? using animals for research …? ('Dissection' p. 9) What responsibilities do we have towards animals? ('The Meadow Mouse' p. 12) Can you ever own a creature? ('The Early Purges' p. 7 and 'The Arrival of the Bee Box' p. 20)

What do you think of factory farming methods? Are we right to rear and kill animals for food? ('The Best Beast …' p. 18)

Drama

Some of the poems and pictures in this section might suggest situations and themes for improvisation. You might be able to develop something from the following brief ideas:

Being in captivity – a caged animal? … a prisoner in jail? … a slave? …

Being hunted – a man on the run?

Going to see the rabbit – a group improvisation on Alan Brownjohn's poem on p. 10.

Carl Sandburg on p. 3 says 'I got a zoo, I got a menagerie inside my ribs …' Look again at 'Wilderness' and see if you can find the creatures in yourself. Animal masks might help you.

Activities

making a folder or display

Collect together the following:

some pictures of animals which you find particularly interesting – your own photographs or drawings, cut-outs from colour supplements, tracings from books;

as much information as you can from library books and wild life magazines about the animals of which you have pictures;

a short anthology of your own poems and stories perhaps suggested by some of the animal poems and pictures in this book or by the pictures and information you have discovered for yourself.

Decide how to set out all this material – a four-page magazine? a display to be put up on the wall of your classroom? Why not work in pairs or small groups?

You will need sugar paper, plain and lined paper, tracing paper, glue, sellotape, scissors.

Bringing creatures into the classroom

This can provide problems of transport and care of the creatures during the rest of the day but with a little thought and planning a group of you could arrange with your teacher to run a series of lessons in which you bring a different creature each time. The biology teacher may be able to help you as well and may perhaps lend you gerbils, frogs, mice and rats for observation.

There will be plenty to talk about and if you bring anything into the classroom, be ready to tell the others about what you have brought.

When you have creatures actually in front of you, it is much easier to write vividly about them because you can *see* the different colours, shapes and details, and the words come more readily into your mind.

Notebook

Observe your own pet closely and jot down impressions of its appearance, behaviour and character.

Look closely at insect life on a patch of earth, on a windowpane or a spider's web. Make notes.

Sit quietly in a park or garden and try to note all the creatures of which you are aware. Describe their appearance and the way they move.

There may be a pond at your school or near your home. You could observe many creatures here – frogs, fish, dragonflies, beetles and jot down notes about them.

If there is a pet shop nearby you could perhaps visit it and build up some notes on the sights, sounds and smells which help to create the atmosphere of the shop.

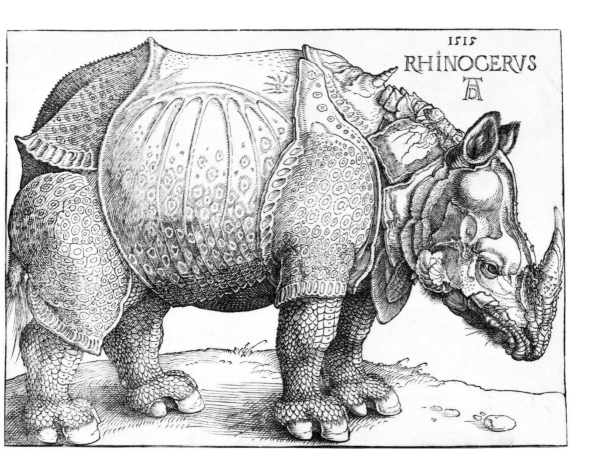

YU

Metaphors

I'm a riddle in nine syllables,
An elephant, a ponderous house,
A melon strolling on two tendrils.
O red fruit, ivory, fine timbers!
This loaf's big with its yeasty rising.
Money's new-minted in this fat purse.
I'm a means, a stage, a cow in calf.
I've eaten a bag of green apples,
Boarded the train there's no getting off.

Sylvia Plath

Morning Song

Love set you going like a fat gold watch.
The midwife slapped your footsoles, and your bald cry
Took its place among the elements.

Our voices echo, magnifying your arrival. New statue.
In a drafty museum, your nakedness
Shadows our safety. We stand round blankly as walls.

I'm no more your mother
Than the cloud that distils a mirror to reflect its own slow
Effacement at the wind's hand.

All night your moth-breath
Flickers among the flat pink roses. I wake to listen:
A far sea moves in my ear.

One cry, and I stumble from bed, cow-heavy and floral
In my Victorian nightgown.
Your mouth opens clean as a cat's. The window square

Whitens and swallows its dull stars. And now you try
Your handful of notes;
The clear vowels rise like balloons.

Sylvia Plath

Baby's Drinking Song

*for a baby learning for the first time
to drink from a cup (Vivace)*

Sip a little
Sup a little
From your little
Cup a little
Sup a little
Sip a little
Put it to your
Lip a little
Tip a little
Tap a little
Not into your
Lap or it'll
Drip a little
Drop a little
On the table
Top a little.

JAMES KIRKUP

A Child Half-asleep

Stealthily parting the small-hours silence,
a hardly-embodied figment of his brain
comes down to sit with me
as I work late.
Flat-footed, as though his legs and feet
were still asleep.

On a stool,
staring into the fire,
his dummy dangling.

Fire ignites the small coals of his eyes;
it stares back through the holes
into his head, into the darkness.

I ask what woke him.

'A wolf dreamed me,' he says.

TONY CONNOR

Children's Song

We live in our own world,
A world that is too small
For you to stoop and enter
Even on hands and knees,
The adult subterfuge.
And though you probe and pry
With analytic eye,
And eavesdrop all our talk
With an amused look,
You cannot find the centre
Where we dance, where we play,
Where life is still asleep
Under the closed flower,
Under the smooth shell
Of eggs in the cupped nest
That mock the faded blue
Of your remoter heaven.

R S THOMAS

Warning to Children

Children, if you dare to think
Of the greatness, rareness, muchness,
Fewness of this precious only
Endless world in which you say
You live, you think of things like this:
Blocks of slate enclosing dappled
Red and green, enclosing tawny
Yellow nets, enclosing white
And black acres of dominoes,
Where a neat brown paper parcel
Tempts you to untie the string.
In the parcel a small island,
On the island a large tree,
On the tree a husky fruit.
Strip the husk and pare the rind off:
In the kernel you will see
Blocks of slate enclosed by dappled
Red and green, enclosed by tawny
Yellow nets, enclosed by white
And black acres of dominoes,
Where the same brown paper parcel –
Children, leave the string alone!
For who dares undo the parcel
Finds himself at once inside it,
On the island, in the fruit,
Blocks of slate about his head,
Finds himself enclosed by dappled
Green and red, enclosed by yellow
Tawny nets, enclosed by black
And white acres of dominoes,
With the same brown paper parcel
Still unopened on his knee.
And, if he then should dare to think
Of the fewness, muchness, rareness,
Greatness of this endless only
Precious world in which he says
He lives – he then unties the string.

ROBERT GRAVES

29

To My Daughter

Bright clasp of her whole hand around my finger,
My daughter, as we walk together now.
All my life I'll feel a ring invisibly
Circle this bone with shining: when she is grown
Far from today as her eyes are far already.

STEPHEN SPENDER

At Seven a Son

In cold weather on a
garden swing, his legs
in wellingtons rising over
the winter rose trees

he sits serenely
smiling like a Thai
his coat open, his gloves
sewn to the flapping sleeves

his thin knees working
with his arms
folded about the
metal struts

as he flies up
(his hair like long
black leaves) he
lies back freely

astonished in
sunshine as serious
as a stranger he is
a bird in his own thought.

ELAINE FEINSTEIN

My Parents Kept Me

My parents kept me from children who were rough
Who threw words like stones and who wore torn clothes.
Their thighs showed through rags. They ran in the street
And climbed cliffs and stripped by the country streams.

I feared more than tigers their muscles like iron
Their jerking hands and their knees tight on my arms.
I feared the salt coarse pointing of those boys
Who copied my lisp behind me on the road.

They were lithe, they sprang out behind hedges
Like dogs to bark at my world. They threw mud
While I looked the other way, pretending to smile.
I longed to forgive them, but they never smiled.

How to catch Tiddlers
(*for Stephen*)

Watch the net drift. Grey tides
Mingle what purposes your eye supposed
But watch the net. There is no fish
Only the net, the way it moves. There is no fish,
Forget the fish. The net is spread
And moving. Steer gently. Keep the hand
Pressured constantly against the stream.
There is no catch now, only the net
And your pressure and your poise. Below,
Ignore the pebbles and the promising weed
Mooning over its secrets. There is just the net,
The hand, and, now, near an old glance somewhere,
A sleek shape holding its body constant,
Firm in its fluid world. Move on. Watch
Only the net. You are a hand only,
Steering, controlling. Now look.
Inside that silent bulge the shape
Breaks black and firm. You may rise,
You may rise now – the deftest
Turn of wrist will do it. Your hand
Crude again can support the cling of mesh.
You can relax, coldly note
The titchy black squirm. You have achieved.
Commit success to jamjars. Lean again.
Dip the slack net. Let it belly.

BRIAN JONES

Death of a Naturalist

All year the flax-dam festered in the heart
Of the townland; green and heavy headed
Flax had rotted there, weighted down by huge sods.
Daily it sweltered in the punishing sun.
Bubbles gargled delicately, bluebottles
Wove a strong gauze of sound around the smell.
There were dragon-flies, spotted butterflies,
But best of all was the warm thick slobber
Of frogspawn that grew like clotted water
In the shade of the banks. Here, every spring
I would fill jampotfuls of the jellied
Specks to range on window-sills at home,
On shelves at school, and wait and watch until
The fattening dots burst into nimble –
Swimming tadpoles. Miss Walls would tell us how
The daddy frog was called a bullfrog
And how he croaked and how the mammy frog
Laid hundreds of little eggs and this was
Frogspawn. You could tell the weather by frogs too
For they were yellow in the sun and brown
In rain.

      Then one hot day when fields were rank
With cowdung in the grass the angry frogs
Invaded the flax-dam; I ducked through hedges
To a coarse croaking that I had not heard
Before. The air was thick with a bass chorus.
Right down the dam gross-bellied frogs were cocked
On sods; their loose necks pulsed like sails. Some hopped:
The slap and plop were obscene threats. Some sat
Poised like mud grenades, their blunt heads farting.
I sickened, turned, and ran. The great slime kings
Were gathered there for vengeance and I knew
That if I dipped my hand the spawn would clutch it.

SEAMUS HEANEY

The Rag Doll to the Heedless Child

I love you
with my linen heart.

You cannot
know how these

rigid, lumpy arms
shudder in your grasp,

or what
tears dam up against

these blue eye-smudges at
your capriciousness.

At night I watch you sleep;
you'll never know

how I thrust my face
into the stream

of your warm breath;
and how

love-words choke me behind
this sewn-up mouth.

DAVID HARSENT

Death of God

I have just hung my teddy bear.
I don't know why
Or what motives I had,
I just, hung him.
Before, he just lay there.
Stuffed and vile;
Seeing inside of me, and
Laughing.
Laughing at me, because I,
I was human.
That's why I hung him.
Because I was human,
But no longer;
I have hung him.
So he has won.

GRAHAM WALLEY

Micky Thumps

As I was going down Treak Street
For half a pound of treacle,
Who should I meet but my old friend Micky Thumps.
He said to me, 'Wilt thou come to our wake?'
I thought a bit,
I thought a bit,
I said I didn't mind;
So I went.

As I was sitting on our doorstep
Who should come by but my old friend Micky Thumps' brother.
He said to me, 'Wilt thou come to our house?
Micky is ill.'
I thought a bit,
I thought a bit,
I said I didn't mind:
So I went.

And he were ill:
He were gradely ill.
He said to me,
'Wilt thou come to my funeral, mon, if I die?'
I thought a bit,
I thought a bit,
I said I didn't mind:
So I went.

And it *were* a funeral.
Some stamped on his grave:
Some spat on his grave:
But I scraped my eyes out for my old friend Micky Thumps.

ANON

Who Do You Think You Are?

Who do you think you are
and where do you think you came from?
From toenails to the hair of your head you are
mixed of the earth, of the air,
Of compounds equal to the burning gold and ame-
thyst lights of the Mountains of the Blood of
Christ at Santa Fé.
Listen to the laboratory man tell what you are
made of, man, listen while he takes you apart.
Weighing 150 pounds you hold 3,500 cubic feet of
gas – oxygen, hydrogen, nitrogen.
From the 22 pounds and 10 ounces of carbon in
you is the filling for 9,000 lead pencils.
In your blood are 50 grains of iron and in the rest
of your frame enough iron to make a spike
that would hold your weight.
From your 50 ounces of phosphorous could be made
800,000 matches and elsewhere in your physical
premises are hidden 60 lumps of sugar, 20 tea-
spoons of salt, 38 quarts of water, two ounces
of lime, and scatterings of starch, chloride of
potash, magnesium, sulphur, hydrochloric acid.
You are a walking drug store and also a cosmos and
a phantasmagoria treading a lonesome valley,
one of the people, one of the minions and
myrmidons who would like an answer to the
question, 'Who and what are you?'
One of the people seeing sun, fog, zero weather,
seeing fire, flood, famine, having meditations
On fish, birds, leaves, seeds,
Skins and shells emptied of living form,
The beautiful legs of Kentucky thoroughbreds
And the patience of army mules.

CARL SANDBURG

Thoughts   Excuse me, isn't that you I see concealed underneath there
Inside the shield, or conning tower, of your head,
Your eyes looking out of the perforations in your flesh?
How can you think you can see from out of liquid, anyway?
      Are rain puddles watching me even now,
And can ducts which punctuate the underground of a field
Examine it at will for buried treasure? Is the rain outside your
      window a voyeur, then? Deep down under all that, though,
Underneath the liquids and the various unobservant stuffs
There is a spirit, shifting around from foot to foot.

MICHAEL BENEDIKT

37

The Cauliflower

I wanted to be a cauliflower,
all brain and ears,
thinking on the origin of gardens
and the divinity of him
who carefully binds my leaves.

With my blind roots touched
by the songs of the worms,
and my rough throat throbbing
with strange, vegetable sounds,
perhaps I'd feel the parting stroke
of a butterfly's wing . . .

Not like my cousins, the cabbages,
whose heads, tightly folded,
see and hear nothing of this world,
dreaming only on the yellow
and green magnificence
that is hardening within them.

JOHN HAINES

Fledglings

FOR RUTH GAYLE CUNNINGHAM
The twelfth grade at St Joseph's High School
in Jackson, Mississippi

As I talk to these children hovering on the verge
Of man and woman, I remember the hanging back
Of my own fledgling, the alternate terror and joke
A child invokes, its claws frozen on the nest-edge.

Fly, I hear myself say now, though they're not my young,
And suddenly I see they are heavy as stones –
I see we are all of us heavy as stones –
How many years is it now I've been falling?

Then two of them, a thin, overbright white
Boy and a slower, steadier Negro girl,
Striking out, each make a fluttering whirl
And I know those two have already dreamt of the flight.

Oh, now the whole classroom is beating leaky wings
As if flying were a mere child's pantomime.
What a moment it is, what a mortal time –
Is there any plummet or flight as sheer as the fledgling's?

WILLIAM MEREDITH

38

Dream of the Cardboard Lover

She fell away from her earthly husband;
it was night in the city
and a dim lamp shone.

The street seemed empty and silent,
but on the pavement before her
lay something weakly flapping.

She bent over and saw in it
the shape of a man, but he
was flattened and thin like a carton.

She picked him up, and looking
into those battered eyes,
she thought she knew him, and cried:

'We sat together in school, long ago,
you were always the one I loved!'

And the cardboard hero shed a paper tear
as he leaned against her
in the dreamlight,
growing dimmer and dimmer.

JOHN HAINES

Dream Variation

To fling my arms wide
In some place of the sun,
To whirl and to dance
Till the white day is done.
Then rest at cool evening
Beneath a tall tree
While night comes on gently,
    Dark like me –
That is my dream!

To fling my arms wide
In the face of the sun,

Dance! whirl! whirl!
Till the quick day is done
Rest at pale evening …
A tall, slim tree …
Night coming tenderly,
    Black like me.

LANGSTON HUGHES

First Ice

A girl freezes in a telephone booth.
In her draughty overcoat she hides
A face all smeared
In tears and lipstick.

She breathes on her thin palms.
Her fingers are icy. She wears earrings.

She'll have to go home alone, alone,
Along the icy street.

First ice. It is the first time.
The first ice of telephone phrases.

Frozen tears glitter on her cheeks –
The first ice of human hurt.

ANDREY VOZNESENSKY

40

Idyll

I was drawing water from the well
When suddenly he looked at me –
I was so moved
That I let slip the rope.

TRADITIONAL AFRICAN

Love Poem

I live in you, you live in me;
We are two gardens haunted by each other.
Sometimes I cannot find you there,
There is only the swing creaking, that you have just left,
Or your favourite book beside the sundial.

DOUGLAS DUNN

Fifteen Line Sonnet in Four Parts

I

When we talk, I imagine silence
Beyond the intervalling words: a space
Empty of all but ourselves there, face to face,
Away from others, alone in the intense
Light or dark, it would not matter which.

II

But where a room envelopes us, one heart,
Our bodies, locked together, prove apart
Unless we change them back again to speech.

III

Close to you here, looking at you, I see
Beyond your eyes looking back, that second you
Of whom the outward semblance is the image –
The inward being where the name springs true.

IV

Today, left only with a name, I rage,
Willing these lines – willing a name to be
Flesh, on the blank unanswering page.

STEPHEN SPENDER

Visiting Miss Emily

When you visit Aunt Em you must whistle
Through railings, and her face will glide
Like a slow white moon to the window-space.

Then you must wait patiently
By the bruised door – (put your ear
Against it, you will hear how slow she comes).

When it opens, say with unusual breeziness
How are you then? but don't listen
For an answer. Instead, go down

Stairs murky as a lost century
And emerge in her underground cavern
Where a cat will panic in the darkness.

There, make as much noise as you can –
Hum, whistle, scrape a chair – before
She enters with that curious and catching malady

Of never having been or done anything.
While you stay, be on your guard.
She is a siren, although she weighs five stone

From some illness she has never recovered from,
Although her hair is thin and lank as a washing-up rag,
Although she keeps a finger crooked to stop a ring falling off.

Soon she will be capering for you, telling stories
Of how during the war she'd dive under the bed
So that the falling bomb would bounce back from the springs;

Of how the sole stripped from her shoe, and she walked
A mile sliding her foot to stop the cod's-mouth flap –
She flickers to life with visits: she forgets,

And soon you'll be groaning and wheezing, helpless.
But keep your wits about you; remember she
Is your kin. Haven't you seen somewhere

That paleness of eyes? that pallor of cheeks?
Haven't you known what it is to slump like that?
Isn't this cavern familiar? and the filtered daylight?

Wish her goodbye. Kiss her cheek as if it were lovely.
Thank her for the soft biscuits and the rancid butter.
Then straighten your tie, pull your cuffs square,

Think of tomorrow as a day when the real begins
With its time and teabreaks. Tell her you'll
Visit her again sometime, one quiet Sunday.

BRIAN JONES

Crabbed Age and Youth

Crabbed Age and Youth
Cannot live together:
Youth is full of pleasance,
Age is full of care;
Youth like summer morn,
Age like winter weather;
Youth like summer brave,
Age like winter bare.
Youth is full of sport,
Age's breath is short;
Youth is nimble, Age is lame;
Youth is hot and bold,
Age is weak, and cold;
Youth is wild, and Age is tame.
Age, I do abhor thee;
Youth, I do adore thee;
O, my Love, my Love is young!
Age, I do defy thee:
O, sweet shepherd, hie thee!
For methinks thou stay'st too long.

WILLIAM SHAKESPEARE

The Old Couple

The old couple in the brand-new bungalow,
Drugged with the milk of municipal kindness,
Fumble their way to bed. Oldness at odds
With newness, they nag each other to show
Nothing is altered, despite the strangeness
Of being divorced in sleep by twin-beds,
Side by side like the Departed, above them
The grass-green of candlewick bedspreads.

In a dead neighbourhood, where it is rare
For hooligans to shout or dogs to bark,
A footfall in the quiet air is crisper
Than home-made bread; and the budgerigar
Bats an eyelid, as sensitive to disturbance
As a distant needle is to an earthquake
In the Great Deep, then balances in sleep.
It is silence keeps the old couple awake.

Too old for loving now, but not for love,
The old couple lie, several feet apart,
Their chesty breathing like a muted duet
On wind instruments, trying to think of
Things to hang on to, such as the tinkle
That a budgerigar makes when it shifts
Its feather weight from one leg to another,
The way, on windy nights, linoleum lifts.

F PRATT GREEN

44

Old People

Nowadays everybody wants to be young,
so much so, that even the young are old with the effort
    of being young.
As for those over fifty, either they rush forward in
    self-assertion
fearful to behold,
or they bear everybody a grim and grisly grudge
because of their own fifty or sixty or seventy or eighty
    summers.
As if it's my fault that the old girl is seventy-seven!

                  D H LAWRENCE

Talking points

1) In this group of poems and pictures we have tried to capture something of the process of growing up – from babyhood, through childhood and adolescence and finally, in contrast, we have printed a few poems about old age.

What do you remember about your earliest years?

Which of you can go back furthest?

Does one incident stand out clearly and sharply in your memory?

Are there any similarities in the things each of you remembers? Are they sad or happy or frightening?

Can you distinguish what you were told by your parents from what *you* actually recall?

Perhaps you could share your memories with your classmates by dividing up into small groups for discussion. Afterwards you may have some ideas which you can write down.

2) What do you feel about the attitude expressed in D. H. Lawrence's poem 'Old People' on p. 45? As before, it is probably best to discuss this in small groups and to ask yourselves –

What do you regard as 'old'?

What contacts does each of you have with old people in your area?

How much is the old age pension worth? How do you think the pension money breaks down into rent, food, clothes, fuel etc.?

Do pensioners have as much pocket money as you?

Activities

1) PARENTS AND CHILDREN

a) Browse through the poems about parents and young children on pp. 26–31 for a few minutes and then the class could spend some time reading the poems out loud and perhaps commenting on them and the pictures.

b) *A short piece of writing*

After you have read the poems, choose the one you like the best and write a paragraph or two saying what you like about it. You may want to include the thoughts and ideas the poem contains, the pictures it creates in you mind's eye, any words, phrases or comparisons which appeal to you ... Perhaps twenty minutes.

c) *Individual or group activities*

As a follow-up piece of work, choose one of the activities below to work on singly or in a group.

i) Take one of the poems as a starting point for drama. Childhood nightmares? ... New baby in the family? ... Family outing or disagreement? ...

ii) Write your own poem suggested by one of the poems or pictures; or find your own picture on this theme of parents and children and write about it. Present your work as a display or in folder form; illustrate with your own drawing or collage.

(You will need sugar paper, some extra pictures from colour supplements or magazines, glue, scissors, etc.)

iii) Try to write a sequel to one of the poems; for example, 'Father Half-Asleep' or 'Warning to Parents' or 'To My Mother'.

iv) Discussion group: re-read the poems which have had most effect on you.

Talk about the feelings that these parents have for their children.

What are the emotional demands made by young children?

What might be the rewards from the parents' point of view?

To give a focus to your discussion we suggest that you either make a tape recording of your talk, or write up individual reports of your different views.

2) Look at Brian Jones's poem 'How to Catch Tiddlers' on p. 32. Choose something practical that *you* know how to do and jot down some notes and ideas. Perhaps you could write your own poem 'How to make ...' or 'How to catch ...'

3) The poems about childhood toys on p. 34 may have reminded you of your own toys. They may be kicking around in a cupboard, handed on to younger brothers or sisters, still (secretly?) cherished, or just dimly remembered. Choose your favourite, describe it in as close a detail as you can, recording your feelings about it as you do so.

Project

AUTOBIOGRAPHY

Sandburg asks the question, 'Who do you think you are?' (p. 36). He suggests one way of looking at yourself. Well, who *do* you think you are? A physical description is a start – five feet five with brown hair and blue eyes. But is it *you*? What makes you unique?

Compile a folder called 'Me' or 'My Life' in which you aim to include the main things that have happened to you and your family. Here are some headings which might jog your memory:

Earliest memories: you may have talked about these already so it should be easy to start writing.

People and incidents at junior school.

Holidays.

Former friends; friends you have kept.

The move to secondary school.

Now – likes, dislikes, appearances, the way you dress and talk, what worries you, where you live.

Your hopes for the future.

You could make this into quite a large project by designing a proper folder and dividing the episodes of your life into different chapters. You might be able to devise a family tree and to obtain some old photographs from home.

Vary the writing as much as possible. There is opportunity to write in diary form, poems, stories both true and imagined, factual accounts, interviews, playlets.

The WORLD around YOU

Winter

Green Mistletoe!
Oh, I remember now
A dell of snow,
Frost on the bough;
None there but I:
Snow, snow, and a wintry sky.

None there but I,
And footprints one by one,
Zigzaggedly,
Where I had run;
Where shrill and powdery
A robin sat in the tree.

And he whistled sweet;
And I in the crusted snow
With snow-clubbed feet
Jigged to and fro,
Till, from the day,
The rose-light ebbed away.

And the robin flew
Into the air, the air,
The white mist through;
And small and rare
The night-frost fell
Into the calm and misty dell.

And the dusk gathered low,
And the silver moon and stars
On the frozen snow
Drew taper bars,
Kindled winking fires
In the hooded briers.

And the sprawling Bear
Growled deep in the sky;
And Orion's hair
Streamed sparkling by:
But the North sighed low,
'Snow, snow, more snow!'

WALTER DE LA MARE

Winter Moon

Where fields and hollows were,
Ponds, lakes, and meres now stand.
From Warminster to Shaftesbury
The hills are icebergs in an arctic sea.
All's silent, livid, sour
As a sucked coin on the tongue.
The light's a gleam of blades,
Yet brackish; like an x-ray photograph's
Dark-grained dead world
It melts the skin off bone,
And reaching under tumuli
Becomes a hand, fine-fingered,
Bone of ivory and skin of wax,
That fondles dust.
        High up,
Nude moon impassive as a fish's eye,
Has placed its watery mirrors here.
The stars have got their flicknives out.

A sentry, drawing breath, gulps
Nails of frost. The tanks are crouching
Under canvas hoods. Drowned settlements
As stark as tombs.
        Across the road
A truck's upturned,
Its wheels responded to the icy kiss,
The bite now fastening in the driver's throat.
There's something in the pallor of his face,
Turned moonwards nervelessly,
Recalls a radiance
The sea was mad to have
When it laid first an image there,
Still groans about the world to keep
And on occasion gets,
To lie at dawn calm as a corpse.

JEREMY HOOKER

And When the Green Man Comes

The man is clothed
in birchbark,
small birds cling to his limbs
and one builds
a nest in his ear.

The clamor of bedlam
infests his hair, a wind
blowing in his head
shakes down
a thought that turns
to moss and lichen
at his feet.

His eyes are blind
with April,
his breath distilled
of butterflies
and bees, and in his beard
the maggot sings.

He comes again
with litter of chips
and empty cans,
his shoes full of mud and dung;

an army of shedding dogs
attends him,
the valley shudders where
he stands,
           redolent of roses,
exalted in
the streaming rain.

JOHN HAINES

Thaw

Suddenly air is careless, generous,
caressing where it gripped. On lawns
the snowmen shrink to tiny pyramids
their eyes of frizzled coke roll out like tears
the blackbird launches song on running streams
and rising like a tide the grass
wells over snow and leaves it islanded
while hills like withheld waves tremble to move.

Time lives again. There are ripples, rivulets
in lanes and gutters, shimmers across bark;
stones and jutting tree-roots shine, while
the heart that through the rigid months became
a memory of spring, an easy yearning,
must be itself again, trembling, susceptible.

BRIAN JONES

In Nature

Here too are life's victims,
captives of an old umbrella,
lives wrecked
by the lifting of a stone.

Sailors marooned
on the island of a leaf
when their ship
of mud and straw went down.

Explorers lost
among roots and raindrops,
drunkards sleeping it off
in the fields of pollen.

Cities of sand that fall,
dust towers that blow away.
Penal colonies
from which no one returns.

Here too, neighbourhoods
in revolt, revengeful columns;
evenings at the broken wall,
black armies in flight …

JOHN HAINES

Clouds

Sharp showers, bright between. Late in the afternoon, the light and shade being brilliant, snowy blocks of cloud were filing over the sky, and under the sun hanging above and along the earth-line were those multitudinous up-and-down crispy sparkling chains with pearly shadows up to the edges. At sunset, which was in a grey bank with moist gold dabs and racks, the whole round of skyline had level clouds naturally lead-colour but the upper parts ruddled, some more, some less, rosy. Spits or beams braided or built in with slanting pellet flakes made their way. Through such clouds anvil-shaped pink ones and up-blown fleece-of-wool flat-topped dangerous-looking pieces.

G M Hopkins
(From Journal Entry for July 1st 1866)

Summer Waterfall, Glendale

I watch a rock shine black
Behind thin water that falls with a frail sound
To the ferny pool. Elvers are roping upwards,
Tumultuous as hair. The rippling ground
Is elvers only, wriggling from crack to crack.

Above, a blackfaced ram,
Its viking head malevolent on the sky,
Peers down, stamps and is gone. A rowanberry
Skims and swims, a scarlet coracle, by.
Between two stones a grassblade breathes *I am*.

Small insect glitters run
On the water's skin. . . . I turn away and see
Distances looking over each other's shoulders
At a black cliff, a ferny pool and me
And a tress of elvers rippling in the sun.

NORMAN MACCAIG

From Weather Bestiary

Sun
  A hard summer. The month I sat at the rock
  One fish rose, belly up, a dead gleam.

Thunder
  Corn, lobster, fleece hotly harvested – now
  That whale stranded on the blue rock!

Frost
  Stiff windless flower, hearse-blossom,
  Show us the brightness of blood, stars, apples.

Fog
  The sun-dipped isle was suddenly a sheep
  Lost and stupid, a dense wet tremulous fleece.

Snow
  Autumn, a moulted parrot, eyes with terror
  This weird white cat. It drifts the rose-bush under.

GEORGE MACKAY BROWN

A Haiku Yearbook

Snow in January
Looking for ledges
To hide in unmelted.

February evening:
A cold puddle of petrol
Makes its own rainbow.

Wind in March:
No leaves left
For its stiff summons.

April sunlight:
Even the livid bricks
Muted a little.

Wasp in May
Storing his venom
For a long summer.

Morning in June:
On the sea's horizon
A white island, alone.

July evening:
Sour reek of beer
Warm by the river.

August morning:
A squirrel leaps and
Only one branch moves.

September chestnuts:
Falling too early,
Split white before birth.

October garden:
At the top of the tree
A thrush stabs an apple.

November morning:
A whiff of cordite
Caught in the leaf mould.

Sun in December:
In his box of straw
The tortoise wakes.

Anthony Thwaite

53

'Sunday Morning'

Sunday morning

> and the sun
> bawls
> with
> his big mouth

Yachts

> paper triangles
> of white and blue
> crowd the sloping bay
> appearing motionless
> as if stuck there
> by some infant thumb
>
> beneath a shouting sky
>
> upon a painted sea

WES MAGEE

Moorings

In a salt ring of moonlight
The dinghy nods at nothing.
It paws the bright water
And scatters its own shadow
In a false net of light.

A ruined chain lies reptile,
Tied to the ground by grasses.
Two oars, wet with sweet water
Filched from the air, are slanted
From a wrecked lobster creel.

The cork that can't be travels –
Nose of a dog otter.
It's piped at, screamed at, sworn at
By elegant oyster catcher
On furious red legs.

With a sort of idle swaying
The tide breathes in. Harsh seaweed
Uncrackles to its kissing;
The skin of the water glistens;
Rich fat swims on the brine.

And all night in his stable
The dinghy paws bright water,
Restless steeplechaser
Longing to clear the hurdles
That ring the Point of Stoer.

NORMAN MacCAIG

54

Paul Klee 'They're Biting' © SPADEM Paris, 1973

At the Fishhouses

Although it is a cold evening,
down by one of the fishhouses
an old man sits netting,
his net, in the gloaming almost invisible
a dark purple-brown,
and his shuttle worn and polished.
The air smells so strong of codfish
it makes one's nose run and one's eyes water.
The five fishhouses have steeply peaked roofs
and narrow, cleated gangplanks slant up
to storerooms in the gables
for the wheelbarrows to be pushed up and down on.
All is silver: the heavy surface of the sea,
swelling slowly as if considering spilling over,
is opaque, but the silver of the benches,
the lobster pots, and masts, scattered
among the wild jagged rocks,
is of an apparent translucence
like the small old buildings with an emerald moss
growing on their shoreward walls.
The big fish tubs are completely lined
with layers of beautiful herring scales
and the wheelbarrows are similarly plastered
with creamy iridescent coats of mail,
with small iridescent flies crawling on them.
Up on the little slope behind the houses,
set in the sparse bright sprinkle of grass,
is an ancient wooden capstan,
cracked, with two long bleached handles
and some melancholy stains, like dried blood,
where the ironwork has rusted.

The old man accepts a Lucky Strike.
He was a friend of my grandfather.
We talk of the decline in the population
and of codfish and herring
while he waits for a herring boat to come in.
There are sequins on his vest and on his thumb.
He has scraped the scales, the principal beauty,
from unnumbered fish with that black old knife,
the blade of which is almost worn away.
Down at the water's edge, at the place
where they haul up the boats, up the long ramp
descending into the water, thin silver
tree trunks are laid horizontally

across the gray stones, down and down
at intervals of four or five feet.

Cold dark deep and absolutely clear,
element bearable to no mortal,
to fish and to seals ... One seal particularly
I have seen here evening after evening.
He was curious about me. He was interested in music;
like me a believer in total immersion,
so I used to sing him Baptist hymns.
I also sang 'A Mighty Fortress Is Our God.'
He stood up in the water and regarded me
steadily, moving his head a little.
Then he would disappear, then suddenly emerge
almost in the same spot, with a sort of shrug
as if it were against his better judgement.
Cold dark deep and absolutely clear,
the clear gray icy water ... Back, behind us,
the dignified tall firs begin.
Bluish, associating with their shadows,
a million Christmas trees stand
waiting for Christmas. The water seems suspended
above the rounded gray and blue-gray stones.
I have seen it over and over, the same sea, the same,
slightly, indifferently swinging above the stones,
icily free above the stones,
above the stones and then the world.
If you should dip your hand in,
your wrist would ache immediately,
your bones would begin to ache and your hand would burn
as if the water were a transmutation of fire
that feeds on stones and burns with a dark gray flame.
If you tasted it, it would first taste bitter,
then briny, then surely burn your tongue.
It is like what we imagine knowledge to be:
dark, salt, clear, moving, utterly free,
drawn from the cold hard mouth
of the world, derived from the rocky breasts
forever, flowing and drawn, and since
our knowledge is historical, flowing, and flown.

ELIZABETH BISHOP

57

To the Sea

To step over the low wall that divides
Road from concrete walk above the shore
Brings sharply back something known long before –
The miniature gaiety of seasides.
Everything crowds under the low horizon:
Steep beach, blue water, towels, red bathing caps,
The small hushed waves' repeated fresh collapse
Up the warm yellow sand, and further off
A white steamer stuck in the afternoon –

Still going on, all of it, still going on!
To lie, eat, sleep in hearing of the surf
(Ears to transistors, that sound tame enough
Under the sky), or gently up and down
Lead the uncertain children, frilled in white
And grasping at enormous air, or wheel
The rigid old along for them to feel
A final summer, plainly still occurs
As half an annual pleasure, half a rite,

As when, happy at being on my own,
I searched the sand for Famous Cricketers,
Or, farther back, my parents, listeners
To the same seaside quack, first became known.
Strange to it now, I watch the cloudless scene:
The same clear water over smoothed pebbles,
The distant bathers' weak protesting trebles
Down at its edge, and then the cheap cigars,
The chocolate-papers, tea-leaves, and, between

The rocks, the rusting soup-tins, till the first
Few families start the trek back to the cars.
The white steamer has gone. Like breathed-on glass
The sunlight has turned milky. If the worst
Of flawless weather is our falling short,
It may be that through habit these do best,
Coming to water clumsily undressed
Yearly; teaching their children by a sort
Of clowning; helping the old, too, as they ought.

PHILIP LARKIN

The Bonfire

Day by day, day after day, we fed it
With straw, mown grass, shavings, shaken weeds,
The huge flat leaves of umbrella plants, old spoil
Left by the builders, combustible; yet it
Coughed fitfully at the touch of a match,
Flared briefly, spat flame through a few dry seeds
Like a chain of fireworks, then slumped back to the soil
Smouldering and smoky, leaving us to watch

Only a heavy grey mantle without fire.
This glum construction seemed choked at heart,
The coils of newspaper burrowed into its hulk
Led our small flames into the middle of nowhere,
Never touching its centre, sodden with rot.
Ritual petrol sprinklings wouldn't make it start
But swerved and vanished over its squat brown bulk,
Still heavily sullen, grimly determined not

To do away with itself. A whiff of smoke
Hung over it as over a volcano.
Until one night, late, when we heard outside
A crackling roar, and saw the far field look
Like a Gehenna* claiming its due dead.   *hell
The beacon beckoned, fierily aglow
With days of waiting, hiding deep inside
Its bided time, ravenous to be fed.

ANTHONY THWAITE

59

A Heap of Stones

I asked directions
at a farmhouse door:
they pointed to a field
high on the hillside
where they said
the Giant's Grave
stood, and waited,
watching by their gate,
an old man
and his wife, watching
till I turned the road,
wondering perhaps why
a man would climb
half a mountain to see
a heap of stones.

Over the ditch and through
the rising bog spotted
with tiny spits of wild cotton
I moved, a mile
an hour, until the land
below became a mood,
long shadows sweeping
inland, eating light . . .

Armed with bright pictures
of club and claw
I searched until suddenly
it grinned at me:
filling the hole in a crazy hedge
it overflowed into the field –
great tables impaled
upon a pencil of stone;
a tabernacle of ancient death
dug deep as an evil eye
in the skull of the hill.
I banished urgent images
from my downward path and one
by one unclenched
the stone cold fingers round my brain.

RICHARD RYAN

The Hippopotamusman

Into the world of the red glass bus
came a man with a face like a hippopotamus

Grotesqueeruptions made horrific
an otherwise normal ugly face
Wartsscrambled over his head
peeping between thin twigs of dry hair
like pink shiny sunsets
Hanging below the neckline
like grapes festering on a vine
And when he blinked
you could glimpse the drunken dance
in the whites of his eyes
like the flash of underpants
through unbuttoned trouserflies

Had the passengers been in groups
there might have been laughter
But they were all singles
and turning their faces to the windows
did not see the view
but behind the privacy of eyelids
had a mental spew

Limpinggropingly looking for a place
went the substandard man
with the hunchbacked face
and finding one sat
and beholding his mudstudded boots
the hippopotamusman
wondered whether it was wednesday.

ROGER McGOUGH

I Return to the Place I was Born

From my youth up I never liked the city.
I never forgot the mountains where I was born.
The world caught me and harnessed me
And drove me through dust, thirty years away from home.
Migratory birds return to the same tree.
Fish find their way back to the pools where they were hatched.
I have been over the whole country,
And have come back at last to the garden of my childhood.
My farm is only ten acres.
The farm house has eight or nine rooms.
Elms and willows shade the back garden.
Peach trees stand by the front door.
The village is out of sight.
You can hear dogs bark in the alleys,
And cocks crow in the mulberry trees.
When you come through the gate into the court
You will find no dust or mess.
Peace and quiet live in every room.
I am contented to stay here the rest of my life.
At last I have found myself.

T'AO YUAN MING
(*Trans. K Rexroth*)

On Roofs of Terry Street

Television aerials, Chinese characters
In the lower sky, wave gently in the smoke.

Nest-building sparrows peck at moss,
Urban flora and fauna, soft, unscrupulous.

Rain drying on the slates shines sometimes.
A builder is repairing someone's leaking roof,

He kneels upright to rest his back,
His trowel catches the light and becomes precious.

DOUGLAS DUNN

The Place's Fault

Once, after a rotten day at school –
Sweat on my fingers, pages thumbed with smears,
Cane smashing down to make me keep them neat –
I blinked out to the sunlight and the heat
And stumbled up the hill, still swallowing tears.
A stone hissed past my ear – 'Yah! gurt fat fool!'

Some urchins waited for me by my gate.
I shouted swear-words at them, walked away.
'Yeller,' they yelled, 'e's yeller!' And they flung
Clods, stones, bricks – anything to make me run.
I ran, all right, up hill all summer day
With 'yeller' in my ears. 'I'm not, I'm not!'

Another time, playing too near the shops –
Oddly, no doubt, I'm told I was quite odd,
Making, no doubt, a noise – a girl in slacks
Came out and told some kids 'Run round the back,
Bash in his back door, smash up his back yard,
And if he yells I'll go and fetch the cops.'

And what a rush I had to lock those doors
Before that rabble reached them! What desire
I've had these twenty years to lock away
That place where fingers pointed out my play,
Where even the grass was tangled with barbed wire,
Where through the streets I waged continual wars!

We left (it was a temporary halt)
The knots of ragged kids, the wired-off beach,
Faces behind the blinds. I'll not return;
There's nothing there I haven't had to learn,
And I've learned nothing that I'd care to teach –
Except that I know it was the place's fault.

PHILIP HOBSBAUM

From the Night Window

The night rattles with nightmares.
Children cry in the close-packed houses,
A man rots in his snoring.
On quiet feet, policemen test doors.
Footsteps become people under streetlamps.
Drunks return from parties,
Sounding of empty bottles and old songs.
The young women come home,
The pleasure in them deafens me.
They trot like small horses
And disappear into white beds
At the edge of the night.
All windows open, this hot night,
And the sleepless, smoking in the dark,
Making small red lights at their mouths,
Count the years of their marriages.

DOUGLAS DUNN

Hotel Room, 12th Floor

This morning I watched from here
a helicopter skirting like a damaged insect
the Empire State Building, that
jumbo size dentist's drill, and landing
on the roof of the PanAm skyscraper.
But now midnight has come in
from foreign places. Its uncivilised darkness
is shot at by a million lit windows, all
ups and acrosses.

But midnight is not
so easily defeated. I lie in bed, between
a radio and a television set, and hear
the wildest of warwhoops continually ululating through
the glittering canyons and gulches —
police cars and ambulances racing
to the broken bones, the harsh screaming
from coldwater flats, the blood
glazed on sidewalks.

The frontier is never
somewhere else. And no stockades
can keep the midnight out.

NORMAN MACCAIG

Ballad of the Landlord

Landlord, landlord,
My roof has sprung a leak.
Don't you 'member I told you about it
Way last week?

Landlord, landlord,
These steps is broken down.
When you come up yourself
It's a wonder you don't fall down.

Ten bucks you say I owe you?
Ten bucks you say is due?
Well, that's ten bucks more'n I'll pay you
Till you fix this house up new.

What? You gonna get eviction orders?
You gonna cut off my heat?
You gonna take my furniture and
Throw it in the street?

Um-huh! You talking high and mighty.
Talk on – till you get through.
You ain't gonna be able to say a word
If I land my fist on you.

Police! Police!
Come and get this man!
He's trying to ruin the government
And overturn the land!

Copper's whistle!
Patrol bell!
Arrest.

Precinct station.
Iron cell.
Headlines in press:

Man threatens landlord

Tenant held no bail

Judge gives Negro 90 days in county jail

LANGSTON HUGHES

Discussion and writing

1) On pp. 49–52 there are poems and pictures about varied seasons and times of year. What is your favourite time of year? Why? Jot down quickly some of the things that make it so. Talk about this with other members of the class. Do your ideas agree or not? You could then write about your favourite season in more finished form. Perhaps you could find a picture to accompany what you have written; or, better still, draw one yourself.

2) 'It was the place's fault' says Philip Hobsbaum in his poem on p. 64. Does where you live affect who you are? What do you like and dislike most about where you live? Where would you most like to live if you had your choice?

3) Living anywhere for a little while, we begin to take it for granted. 'There's nothing interesting about *my* street' you might say. Isn't there? Perhaps you could write about it – the look of the houses, the sort of people who live there, the noises (and smells) that make it different, the neighbours. Talk around the topic first.

4) Richard Ryan's poem 'A Heap of Stones' tells of a visit to a lonely pre-historic stone circle in the hills. There is something frightening in the atmosphere of the place. Do you know anywhere that has this power to frighten? What is the loneliest place you have ever been in? – on a moorland, or a deserted beach; perhaps a street late at night; in a small boat or swimming some way out to sea? Talk about it and see if you have the basis for a written piece.

5) 'I Return to the Place I was Born' p. 63. Have you ever returned to some-where after a long absence …? a place where you once lived, a previous school, somewhere you visited once before on holiday? Were things as you had remembered them? Had the place changed or had you? Try to write about your feelings.

6) Look again at George Mackay Brown's poem on p. 52. What is a bestiary? Perhaps you could continue the poem with your own verses on wind, rain, hail, lightning, drizzle …

7) Anthony Thwaite's poem on p. 53 is composed of twelve haiku verses. A haiku, as you may already know, is a Japanese verse form ideally, thought not necessarily, composed of 17 syllables arranged over three lines in the pattern 5, 7, 5. Try to write your own haiku sequence for the year, the four seasons, or for the days of the week.

Project

Making a Newspaper
Divide up into groups of four and regard yourselves as groups of journalists who are to report on the world around you. Each group should aim to produce

its own newspaper: you decide the title, column lay-out, page size and so on, and then share out the writing and illustration amongst the four of you.

Take the people, scenes, incidents and ideas from the poems and pictures in this section as a basis for your writing. For example, if you read 'Ballad of a Landlord' (p. 67) carefully, you could invent your own account of this situation using one of the headlines at the end of the poem as your starter; or, less dramatically, you could imagine a mystery story suggested by 'A Heap of Stones' (p. 60) and the photograph alongside it; you could write humorously about the hippopotamusman (p. 62), or simply give an account of the local weather suggested by one of the first four poems in the section.

Aim at as much variety in the tone of your writing as you can manage. Try to present your newspaper as realistically as possible: you will have to plan the lay-out of each page carefully before you actually begin to write up the finished paper.

FIVE POETS

Ted Hughes

A Yorkshireman whose father was a carpenter, Ted Hughes was born in 1930 at Mytholmroyd. When he was seven the family moved to the mining town of Mexborough where his parents ran a newsagent's and tobacconist's shop. After completing his National Service he went to Cambridge and subsequently worked in a number of jobs before becoming a teacher. His wife was the American poet Sylvia Plath.

His poems are often dark and violent, and images of physical power frequently recur. His world of nature asks no quarter and gives none – even the snowdrop is metallic and brutal: the slow grinding of the evolutionary process and the battle for survival dominate. The arch-survivor, man, is seen in the form of Crow – the incorrigible amoral creation who knows how to bend the rules.

In a talk which Ted Hughes recorded for the BBC a few years ago, he began by recalling his childhood love of animals, when as a boy living first in a Pennine valley in West Yorkshire and later in an industrial town in South Yorkshire, he spent a good deal of time hunting and trapping, retrieving birds and animals which his brother shot, fishing in the local canal, and drawing and modelling creatures for his own pictorial zoo. He went on:

... at about fifteen my life grew more complicated and my attitude to animals changed. I accused myself of disturbing their lives. I began to look at them, you see, from their own point of view.

And about the same time I began to write poems. Not animal poems. It was years before I wrote what you could call an animal poem and several more years before it occurred to me that my writing poems might be partly a continuation of my earlier pursuit. Now I have no doubt. The special kind of excitement, the slightly mesmerised and quite involuntary concentration with which you make out the stirrings of a new poem in your mind, then the outline, the mass and colour and clean final form of it, the unique living reality of it in the midst of the general lifelessness, all that is too familiar to mistake. This is hunting and the poem is a new species of creature, a new specimen of the life outside your own ...

Some of (this) may seem a bit obscure to you. How can a poem, for instance, about a walk in the rain, be like an animal? Well, perhaps it cannot look much like a giraffe or an emu or an octopus, or anything you might find in a menagerie. It is better to call it an assembly of living parts moved by a single spirit. The living parts are the words, the images, the rhythms. The spirit is the life which inhabits them when they all work together. It is impossible to say which comes first, parts or spirit. But if any of the parts are dead ... if any of the words, or images or rhythms do not jump to life as you read them ... then the creature is going to be maimed and the spirit sickly. So, as a poet, you have to make sure that all those parts over which you have control, the words and rhythms and images, are alive. That is where the difficulties begin. Yet the rules to begin with are very simple. Words which live are those which we hear, like 'click' or 'chuckle', or which we see, like 'freckled' or 'veined', or which we taste, like 'vinegar' or 'sugar', or touch, like 'prickle' or 'oily', or smell, like 'tar' or 'onion'. Words which belong directly to one of the five senses. Or words which act and seem to use their muscles, like 'flick' or 'balance'.

But immediately things become more difficult. 'Click' not only gives you a sound, it gives you the notion of a sharp movement ... such as your tongue makes in saying 'click'. It also gives you the feel of something light and brittle – like a snapping twig. Heavy things do not click, nor do soft bendable ones. In the same way, tar not only smells strongly. It is sticky to touch, with a particular thick and choking stickiness. Also it moves, when it is soft, like a black snake, and has a beautiful black gloss. So it is with most words. They belong to several of the senses at once, as if each one had eyes, ears and tongue, or ears and fingers and a body to move with. It is this little goblin in a word which is its life and its poetry, and it is this goblin which the poet has to have under control.

Well, you will say, this is hopeless. How do you control all that. When the words are pouring out, how can you be sure that you do not have one of these side meanings of the word 'feathers' stuck up with one of the side meanings of the word 'treacle', a few words later. In bad poetry this is exactly what happens, the words kill each other. Luckily, you do not have to bother about it so long as you do one thing.

That one thing is to imagine what you are writing about. See it and live it. Do not think it up laboriously, as if you were working out mental arithmetic. Just look at it, touch it, smell it, listen to it, turn yourself into it. When you do this, the words look after themselves like magic. If you do this you do not have to bother about commas or full-stops or that sort of thing. You do not look at the words either. You keep your eyes, your ears, your nose, your taste, your touch, your whole being on the thing you are turning into words. The minute you flinch, and take your mind off this thing, and begin to look at the words and worry about them ... then your worry goes into them and they set about killing each other. So you keep going as long as you can, then look back and see what you have written. After a bit of practice, and after telling yourself a few times that you do not care how other people have written about this thing, this is the way you find it; and after telling yourself that you are going to use any old word that comes into your head so long as it seems right at the moment of writing it down, you will surprise yourself. You will read back through what you have written and you will get a shock. You will have captured a spirit, a creature ...

An animal I never succeeded in keeping alive is the fox. I was always frustrated: twice by a farmer, who killed cubs I had caught before I could get to them, and once by a poultry keeper who freed my cub while his dog waited. Years after those events I was sitting up late one snowy night in dreary lodgings in London. I had written nothing for a year or so but that night I got the idea I might write something and I wrote in a few minutes the following poem: the first 'animal' poem I ever wrote. Here it is:

The Thought-Fox

I imagine this midnight moment's forest:
Something else is alive
Beside the clock's loneliness
And this blank page where my fingers move.

Through the window I see no star:
Something more near
Though deeper within darkness
Is entering the loneliness:

Cold, delicately as the dark snow,
A fox's nose touches twig, leaf;
Two eyes serve a movement, that now
And again now, and now, and now

Sets neat prints into the snow
Between trees, and warily a lame
Shadow lags by stump and in hollow
Of a body that is bold to come

Across clearings, an eye,
A widening deepening greenness,
Brilliantly, concentratedly,
Coming about its own business

Till, with a sudden sharp hot stink of fox
It enters the dark hole of the head.
The window is starless still; the clock ticks,
The page is printed.

This poem does not have anything you could easily call a meaning. It is about a fox, obviously enough, but a fox that is both a fox and not a fox. What sort of fox is it that can step right into my head where presumably it still sits ... smiling to itself when the dogs bark. It is both a fox and a spirit. It is a real fox; as I read the poem I see it move, I see it setting its prints, I see its shadow going over the irregular surface of the snow. The words show me all this, bringing it nearer and nearer. It is very real to me. The words have made a body for it and given it somewhere to walk.

(From *Capturing Animals* by Ted Hughes)

The Warm and the Cold

Freezing dusk is closing
  Like a slow trap of steel
On trees and roads and hills and all
  That can no longer feel.
     But the carp is in its depth
      Like a planet in its heaven
     And the badger in its bedding
      Like a loaf in the oven
     And the butterfly in its mummy
      Like a viol in its case
     And the owl in its feathers
      Like a doll in its lace.

Freezing dusk has tightened
  Like a nut screwed tight
On the starry aeroplane
  Of the hurtling night.
     But the trout is in its hole
      Like a giggle in a sleeper.
     The hare strays down the highway
      Like a root going deeper.
     The snail is dry in the outhouse
      Like a seed in a sunflower.
     The owl is pale on the gatepost
      Like a clock on its tower.

Moonlight freezes the shaggy world
  Like a mammoth of ice –
The past and the future
  Are the jaws of a steel vice.
     But the cod is in the tide-rip
      Like a key in a purse.
     The deer are on the bare-blown hill
      Like smiles on a nurse.
     The flies are behind the plaster
      Like the lost score of a jig
     Sparrows are in the ivy-clump
      Like money in a pig.

Such a frost
  The freezing moon
    Has lost her wits.

      A star falls.

The sweating farmers
  Turn in their sleep
    Like oxen on spits.

The Jaguar

The apes yawn and adore their fleas in the sun.
The parrots shriek as if they were on fire, or strut
Like cheap tarts to attract the stroller with the nut.
Fatigued with indolence, tiger and lion

Lie still as the sun. The boa-constrictor's coil
Is a fossil. Cage after cage seems empty, or
Stinks of sleepers from the breathing straw.
It might be painted on a nursery wall.

But who runs like the rest past these arrives
At a cage where the crowd stands, stares, mesmerized,
As a child at a dream, at a jaguar hurrying enraged
Through prison darkness after the drills of his eyes

On a short fierce fuse. Not in boredom –
The eye satisfied to be blind in fire,
By the bang of blood in the brain deaf the ear –
He spins from the bars, but there's no cage to him

More than to the visionary his cell:
His stride is wildernesses of freedom:
The world rolls under the long thrust of his heel.
Over the cage floor the horizons come.

Snowdrop

Now is the globe shrunk tight
Round the mouse's dulled wintering heart.
Weasel and crow, as if moulded in brass,
Move through an outer darkness
Not in their right minds,
With the other deaths. She, too, pursues her ends,
Brutal as the stars of this month,
Her pale head heavy as metal.

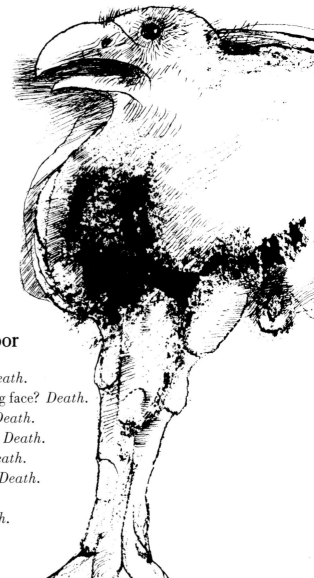

Examination at the Womb Door

Who owns these scrawny little feet? *Death.*
Who owns this bristly scorched-looking face? *Death.*
Who owns these still-working lungs? *Death.*
Who owns this utility coat of muscles? *Death.*
Who owns these unspeakable guts? *Death.*
Who owns these questionable brains? *Death.*
All this messy blood? *Death.*
These minimum-efficiency eyes? *Death.*
This wicked little tongue? *Death.*
This occasional wakefulness? *Death.*

Given, stolen, or held pending trial?
Held.

Who owns the whole rainy, stony earth? *Death.*
Who owns all of space? *Death.*

Who is stronger than hope? *Death.*
Who is stronger than the will? *Death.*
Stronger than love? *Death.*
Stronger than life? *Death.*

But who is stronger than death?
        Me, evidently.

Pass, Crow.

Crow's Song of Himself

When God hammered Crow
He made gold
When God roasted Crow in the sun
He made diamond
When God crushed Crow under weights
He made alcohol
When God tore Crow to pieces
He made money
When God blew Crow up
He made day
When God hung Crow on a tree
He made fruit
When God buried Crow in the earth
He made man
When God tried to chop Crow in two
He made woman
When God said: 'You win, Crow,'
He made the Redeemer.

When God went off in despair
Crow stropped his beak and started in on the two thieves.

King of Carrion

His palace is of skulls.

His crown is the last splinters
Of the vessel of life.

His throne is the scaffold of bones, the hanged thing's
Rack and final stretcher.

His robe is the black of the last blood.

His kingdom is empty –

The empty world, from which the last cry
Flapped hugely, hopelessly away
Into the blindness and dumbness and deafness of the gulf

Returning, shrunk, silent

To reign over silence.

Sylvia Plath

'Certain poems and lines of poetry seem as solid and miraculous to me as church altars or the coronation of queens must seem to people who revere quite different images. I am not worried that poems reach relatively few people. As it is, they go surprisingly far – among strangers, around the world, even. Farther than the words of the classroom teacher or the prescriptions of a doctor; if they are very lucky, farther than a lifetime.' (From 'Context' by Sylvia Plath in *The London Magazine*, Feb. 1962.)

Sylvia Plath died in London in 1963 at the age of 30. She was born in Boston, Massachusetts and educated in the United States, graduating from Smith College in 1955. She came to Britain immediately afterwards to study at Cambridge for the next two years, during which time she met and married Ted Hughes. All of her work was crowded into the short period between her graduation and her death, most of her poems being written in the last three or four years of her life.

Mushrooms

Overnight, very
Whitely, discreetly,
Very quietly

Our toes, our noses
Take hold on the loam,
Acquire the air.

Nobody sees us,
Stops us, betrays us;
The small grains make room.

Soft fists insist on
Heaving the needles,
The leafy bedding,

Even the paving.
Our hammers, our rams,
Earless and eyeless,

Perfectly voiceless,
Widen the crannies,
Shoulder through holes. We

Diet on water,
On crumbs of shadow,
Bland-mannered, asking

Little or nothing.
So many of us!
So many of us!

We are shelves, we are
Tables, we are meek,
We are edible,

Nudgers and shovers
In spite of ourselves.
Our kind multiplies:

We shall by morning
Inherit the earth.
Our foot's in the door.

You're

Clownlike, happiest on your hands,
Feet to the stars, and moon-skulled,
Gilled like a fish. A common-sense
Thumbs-down on the dodo's mode.
Wrapped up in yourself like a spool,
Trawling your dark as owls do.
Mute as a turnip from the Fourth
Of July to All Fools' Day,
O high-riser, my little loaf.

Vague as fog and looked for like mail.
Farther off than Australia.
Bent-backed Atlas, our travelled prawn.
Snug as a bud and at home
Like a sprat in a pickle jug.
A creel of eels, all ripples.
Jumpy as a Mexican bean.
Right, like a well-done sum.
A clean slate, with your own face on.

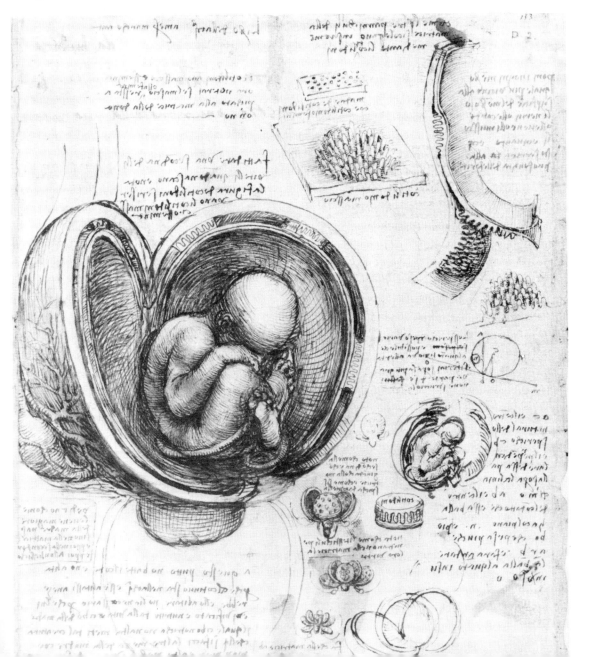

A Winter Ship

At this wharf there are no grand landings to speak of.
Red and orange barges list and blister
Shackled to the dock, outmoded, gaudy,
And apparently indestructible.
The sea pulses under a skin of oil.

A gull holds his pose on a shanty ridgepole,
Riding the tide of the wind, steady
As wood and formal, in a jacket of ashes,
The whole flat harbour anchored in
The round of his yellow eye-button.

A blimp swims up like a day-moon or tin
Cigar over his rink of fishes.
The prospect is dull as an old etching.
They are unloading three barrels of little crabs.
The pier pilings seem about to collapse

And with them that rickety edifice
Of warehouses, derricks, smokestacks and bridges
In the distance. All around us the water slips
And gossips in its loose vernacular,
Ferrying the smells of dead cod and tar.

Farther out, the waves will be mouthing icecakes–
A poor month for park-sleepers and lovers.
Even our shadows are blue with cold.
We wanted to see the sun come up
And are met, instead, by this iceribbed ship,

Bearded and blown, an albatross of frost,
Relic of tough weather, every winch and stay
Encased in a glassy pellicle.
The sun will diminish it soon enough:
Each wave-tip glitters like a knife.

Balloons

Since Christmas they have lived with us,
Guileless and clear,
Oval soul-animals,
Taking up half the space,
Moving and rubbing on the silk

Invisible air drifts,
Giving a shriek and pop
When attacked, then scooting to rest, barely trembling.
Yellow cathead, blue fish —
Such queer moons we live with

Instead of dead furniture!
Straw mats, white walls
And these travelling
Globes of thin air, red, green,
Delighting

The heart like wishes or free
Peacocks blessing
Old ground with a feather
Beaten in starry metals.
Your small

Brother is making
His balloon squeak like a cat.
Seeming to see
A funny pink world he might eat on the other side of it,
He bites,

Then sits
Back, fat jug
Contemplating a world clear as water.
A red
Shred in his little fist.

Seamus Heaney

Seamus Heaney writes: 'Possibly the most relevant fact is the removal from a rural to an urban environment – death of a naturalist, partly. I was born in 1939 on a farm in County Derry and I grew up in a community where traditional methods of farming – horse-ploughs, mowing with scythes, hand-threshing – were still in operation. My father was also a cattle-dealer and I saw much of the cattle-fairs of the Ulster countryside.' His appointment as a university lecturer and the passage of time meant change. '... (the) death of a traditional way of life, and the sense of loss which I experienced in my new academic environment are probably the most pertinent feelings. I am the eldest son of a family of eight children, three of whom still work on the farm.' In 1972 Seamus Heaney left the Queens University of Belfast to live in County Wicklow in the Republic of Ireland, and to devote himself full time to writing. For three years he made his living as a freelance writer. In 1975 he returned to teaching and is now Head of the English Department at a College of Education in Dublin.

Blackberry-Picking

For Philip Hobsbaum

Late August, given heavy rain and sun
For a full week, the blackberries would ripen.
At first, just one, a glossy purple clot
Among others, red, green, hard as a knot.
You ate that first one and its flesh was sweet
Like thickened wine: summer's blood was in it
Leaving stains upon the tongue and lust for
Picking. Then red ones inked up and that hunger
Sent us out with milk-cans, pea-tins, jam-pots
Where briars scratched and wet grass bleached our boots.
Round hayfields, cornfields and potato-drills
We trekked and picked until the cans were full,
Until the tinkling bottom had been covered
With green ones, and on top big dark blobs burned
Like a plate of eyes. Our hands were peppered
With thorn pricks, our palms sticky as Bluebeard's.

We hoarded the fresh berries in the byre.
But when the bath was filled we found a fur,
A rat-grey fungus, glutting on our cache.
The juice was stinking too. Once off the bush
The fruit fermented, the sweet flesh would turn sour.

I always felt like crying. It wasn't fair
That all the lovely canfuls smelt of rot.
Each year I hoped they'd keep, knew they would not.

Digging

Between my finger and my thumb
The squat pen rests; snug as a gun.

Under my window, a clean rasping sound
When the spade sinks into gravelly ground:
My father, digging. I look down

Till his straining rump among the flowerbeds
Bends low, comes up twenty years away
Stooping in rhythm through potato drills
Where he was digging.

The coarse boot nestled on the lug, the shaft
Against the inside knee was levered firmly.
He rooted out tall tops, buried the bright edge deep
To scatter new potatoes that we picked
Loving their cool hardness in our hands.

By God, the old man could handle a spade.
Just like his old man.

My grandfather cut more turf in a day
Than any other man on Toner's bog.
Once I carried him milk in a bottle
Corked sloppily with paper. He straightened up
To drink it, then fell to right away

Nicking and slicing neatly, heaving sods
Over his shoulder, going down and down
For the good turf. Digging.

The cold smell of potato mould, the squelch and slap
Of soggy peat, the curt cuts of an edge
Through living roots awaken in my head.
But I've no spade to follow men like them.

Between my finger and my thumb
The squat pen rests.
I'll dig with it.

The Barn

Threshed corn lay piled like grit of ivory
Or solid as cement in two-lugged sacks.
The musty dark hoarded an armoury
Of farmyard implements, harness, plough-socks.

The floor was mouse-grey, smooth, chilly concrete.
There were no windows, just two narrow shafts
Of gilded motes, crossing, from air-holes slit
High in each gable. The one door meant no draughts

All summer when the zinc burned like an oven.
A scythe's edge, a clean spade, a pitch-fork's prongs:
Slowly bright objects formed when you went in.
Then you felt cobwebs clogging up your lungs

And scuttled fast into the sunlit yard.
And into nights when bats were on the wing
Over the rafters of sleep, where bright eyes stared
From piles of grain in corners, fierce, unblinking.

The dark gulfed like a roof-space. I was chaff
To be pecked up when birds shot through the air-slits.
I lay face-down to shun the fear above.
The two-lugged sacks moved in like great blind rats.

The Forge

All I know is a door into the dark.
Outside, old axles and iron hoops rusting;
Inside, the hammered anvil's short-pitched ring,
The unpredictable fantail of sparks
Or hiss when a new shoe toughens in water.
The anvil must be somewhere in the centre,
Horned as a unicorn, at one end square,
Set there immoveable: an altar
Where he expends himself in shape and music.
Sometimes, leather-aproned, hairs in his nose,
He leans out on the jamb, recalls a clatter
Of hoofs where traffic is flashing in rows;
Then grunts and goes in, with a slam and flick
To beat real iron out, to work the bellows.

Limbo

Fishermen at Ballyshannon
Netted an infant last night
Along with the salmon.
An illegitimate spawning,

A small one thrown back
To the waters. But I'm sure
As she stood in the shallows
Ducking him tenderly

Till the frozen knobs of her wrists
Were as dead as the gravel,
He was a minnow with hooks
Tearing her open.

She waded in under
The sign of her cross.
He was hauled in with the fish.
Now limbo will be

A cold glitter of souls
Through some far briny zone.
Even Christ's palms, unhealed,
Smart and cannot fish there.

Robert Frost

Robert Frost was born in San Fransisco in 1875 and died in 1963. He had some small success with his poems in his teens, graduated in 1895 and entered Harvard two years later. After trying various jobs he moved to Derry, New Hampshire as a farmer and continued to write. In 1912 he sold the farm and sailed for England with his wife and four children. Here he published his first book of verse, which soon won critical acclaim. In 1915 the family returned to America where he wrote and taught for the remainder of his life.

His poems are sometimes deceptively simple in style – characteristically warm, open and honest, often implying a wisdom which seems closely linked to the earth and the rhythms of nature and the soil. Through them all there runs the characteristic Frost voice, colloquial, wry and not without a quiet humour.

The Road Not Taken

Two roads diverged in a yellow wood,
And sorry I could not travel both
And be one traveller, long I stood
And looked down one as far as I could
To where it bent in the undergrowth;

Then took the other, as just as fair,
And having perhaps the better claim,
Because it was grassy and wanted wear;
Though as for that the passing there
Had worn them really about the same,

And both that morning equally lay
In leaves no step had trodden black.
Oh, I kept the first for another day!
Yet knowing how way leads on to way,
I doubted if I should ever come back.

I shall be telling this with a sigh
Somewhere ages and ages hence:
Two roads diverged in a wood, and I –
I took the one less travelled by,
And that has made all the difference.

Design

I found a dimpled spider, fat and white,
On a white heal-all, holding up a moth
Like a white piece of rigid satin cloth –
Assorted characters of death and blight
Mixed ready to begin the morning right,
Like the ingredients of a witches' broth –
A snow-drop spider, a flower like a froth,
And dead wings carried like a paper kite.

What had that flower to do with being white,
The wayside blue and innocent heal-all?
What brought the kindred spider to that height,
Then steered the white moth thither in the night?
What but design of darkness to appal? –
If design govern in a thing so small.

The Runaway

Once when the snow of the year was beginning to fall,
We stopped by a mountain pasture to say, 'Whose colt?'
A little Morgan had one forefoot on the wall,
The other curled at his breast. He dipped his head
And snorted at us. And then he had to bolt.
We heard the miniature thunder where he fled,
And saw him, or thought we saw him, dim and grey,
Like a shadow against the curtain of falling flakes.
'I think the little fellow's afraid of the snow.
He isn't winter-broken. It isn't play
With the little fellow at all. He's running away.
I doubt if even his mother could tell him, "Sakes,
It's only weather." He'd think she didn't know!
Where is his mother? He can't be out alone.'
And now he comes again with clatter of stone,
And mounts the wall again with whited eyes
And all his tail that isn't hair up straight.
He shudders his coat as if to throw off flies.
'Whoever it is that leaves him out so late,
When other creatures have gone to stall and bin,
Ought to be told to come and take him in.'

Lodged

The rain to the wind said,
'You push and I'll pelt.'
They so smote the garden bed
That the flowers actually knelt,
And lay lodged — though not dead.
I know how the flowers felt.

Nothing Gold Can Stay

Nature's first green is gold,
Her hardest hue to hold.
Her early leaf's a flower;
But only so an hour.
Then leaf subsides to leaf.
So Eden sank to grief,
So dawn goes down to day.
Nothing gold can stay.

At Woodward's Gardens

or, Resourcefulness Is More Than Understanding

A boy, presuming on his intellect,
Once showed two little monkeys in a cage
A burning-glass they could not understand
And never could be made to understand.
Words are no good: to say it was a lens
For gathering solar rays would not have helped.
But let him show them how the weapon worked.
He made the sun a pin-point on the nose
Of first one, then the other till it brought
A look of puzzled dimness to their eyes
That blinking could not seem to blink away.
They stood arms laced together at the bars,
And exchanged troubled glances over life.
One put a thoughtful hand up to his nose
As if reminded – or as if perhaps
Within a million years of an idea.
He got his purple little knuckles stung.
The already known had once more been confirmed
By psychological experiment,
And that were all the finding to announce
Had the boy not presumed too close and long.
There was a sudden flash of arm, a snatch,
And the glass was the monkey's, not the boy's.
Precipitately they retired back cage
And instituted an investigation
On their part, though without the needed insight.
They bit the glass and listened for the flavour.
They broke the handle and the binding off it.
Then none the wiser, frankly gave it up,
And having hid it in their bedding straw
Against the day of prisoners' ennui,
Came dryly forward to the bars again
To answer for themselves: Who said it mattered
What monkeys did or didn't understand?
They might not understand a burning-glass.
They might not understand the sun itself.
It's knowing what to do with things that counts.

'Out, Out —'

The buzz saw snarled and rattled in the yard
And made dust and dropped stove-length sticks of wood,
Sweet-scented stuff when the breeze drew across it.
And from there those that lifted eyes could count
Five mountain ranges one behind the other
Under the sunset far into Vermont.
And the saw snarled and rattled, snarled and rattled,
As it ran light, or had to bear a load.
And nothing happened: day was all but done.
Call it a day, I wish they might have said
To please the boy by giving him the half hour
That a boy counts so much when saved from work.
His sister stood beside them in her apron
To tell them 'Supper'. At the word, the saw,
As if to prove saws knew what supper meant,
Leaped out at the boy's hand, or seemed to leap –
He must have given the hand. However it was,
Neither refused the meeting. But the hand!
The boy's first outcry was a rueful laugh,
As he swung toward them holding up the hand
Half in appeal, but half as if to keep
The life from spilling. Then the boy saw all –
Since he was old enough to know, big boy
Doing a man's work, though a child at heart –
He saw all spoiled. 'Don't let him cut my hand off –
The doctor, when he comes. Don't let him, sister!'
So. But the hand was gone already.
The doctor put him in the dark of ether.
He lay and puffed his lips out with his breath.
And then – the watcher at his pulse took fright.
No one believed. They listened at his heart.
Little – less – nothing! – and that ended it.
No more to build on there. And they, since they
Were not the one dead, turned to their affairs.

Spring Pools

These pools that, though in forests, still reflect
The total sky almost without defect,
And like the flowers beside them, chill and shiver,
Will like the flowers beside them soon be gone,
And yet not out by any brook or river,
But up by roots to bring dark foliage on.

The trees that have it in their pent-up buds
To darken nature and be summer woods –
Let them think twice before they use their powers
To blot out and drink up and sweep away
These flowery waters and these watery flowers
From snow that melted only yesterday.

Brian Patten

Brian Patten was born in Liverpool in 1946. At fifteen he joined the local newspaper, but left after spending eighteen months as a reporter. He has published several books of poetry but perhaps the event which brought him his widest audience was the inclusion of a selection of his poems in *The Mersey Sound*, volume ten in the 'Penguin Modern Poets' Series, which also features the work of Adrian Henri and Roger McGough.

You will find that Brian Patten writes in a lighter, more colloquial style than the other poets represented in this section. There is a freshness and humour about his work which is often best seen when the poems are read aloud. Yet, as poems like *Bombscare* and *Mr Jones Takes Over* show, Patten's light-hearted, whimsical style does not preclude thoughtful comment on the concerns of present-day living. Perhaps his informality is the quality which distinguishes him most sharply from the other poets: certainly here is a voice which seems to capture the style and attitude of a significant proportion of young people today.

Little Johnny's Confession

This morning
    being rather young and foolish
    I borrowed a machine gun my father
    had left hidden since the war, went out
    and eliminated a number of small enemies.
    Since then I have not returned home.

This morning
    swarms of police with trackerdogs
    wander about the city
    with my description printed
    on their minds, asking:
    'Have you seen him?
    He is seven years old,
    likes Pluto, Mighty Mouse
    and Biffo the Bear,
    have you seen him, anywhere?'

This morning
    sitting alone in a strange playground
    muttering you've blundered, you've blundered
    over and over to myself
    I work out my next move
    but cannot move.
    The trackerdogs will sniff me out,
    they have my lollipops.

Little Johnny's Final Letter

Mother,
I won't be home this evening, so
don't worry; don't hurry to report me missing.
Don't drain the canals to find me,
I've decided to stay alive, don't
search the woods, I'm not hiding,
simply gone to get myself classified.
Don't leave my shreddies out,
I've done with security.
Don't circulate my photograph to society
I have disguised myself as a man
and am giving priority to obscurity.
It suits me fine;
I have taken off my short trousers
and put on long ones, and
now am going out into the city, so
don't worry; don't hurry to report me missing.

I've rented a room without any curtains
and sit behind the windows growing cold,
heard your plea on the radio this morning,
you sounded sad and strangely old. ...

The Projectionist's Nightmare

This is the projectionist's nightmare:
A bird finds its way into the cinema,
finds the beam, flies down it,
smashes into a screen depicting a garden,
a sunset and two people being nice to each other.
Real blood, real intestines, slither down
the likeness of a tree.
'This is no good,' screams the audience,
'This is not what we came to see.'

Mr Jones Takes Over

Look, the Jones have moved into Paradise!
They've built a house there,
laid down a road or two,
built several yachts for the garden,
two garages, one church with its plastic vicar.

I asked hopefully when the lease would expire.
'We paid in cash,' they smiled.

Bombscare

Without much effort the piece of earth I was sitting on
broke off like fruit-cake from the ground
and drifted out of what we call the world.
Fortunately I had my winter clothes on,
for with every star I pass I'm growing colder,
it's a wonderous and amazing sight to see them pass
like bubbles in clear water.

I did not set out on this journey alone;
there were some picnickers here but they seemed
to shrink and disappear. Funny, they seemed
quite like myself at first.

Still there are some creatures here,
rabbits, squirrels, a few gibbering hares,
we join in a circle to keep warm
and as each fails and dies I take their fur
and bury myself beneath it.

If you see my shadow drift across your lawn,
the shadow of a man in winter clothes
sitting on a lump of soil,
you're bound to be amazed, but do not phone
an ambulance or a fire-brigade;
even helicopters could not reach me,
and spaceships I fear are too expensive.

Now I've grown used to it and as I said
with every star I pass I'm growing colder;
it's funny how the worlds are made
and how some pass through bombscare to laughter.

A Small Dragon

I've found a small dragon in the woodshed.
Think it must have come from deep inside a forest
because it's damp and green and leaves
are still reflecting in its eyes.

I fed it on many things, tried grass,
the roots of stars, hazel-nut and dandelion,
but it stared up at me as if to say, I need
food you can't provide.

It made a nest among the coal,
not unlike a bird's but larger,
it is out of place here
and is quite silent.

If you believed in it I would come
hurrying to your house to let you share my wonder,
but I want instead to see
if you yourself will pass this way.

This section provides those of you who would like to do so with a chance to begin a study in depth of a particular writer. The poems selected to represent each of the five poets are, of course, only a small part of their output and, as three of them are still writing, this section can only act as an introduction to their work.

Group discussion (*five groups, one on each poet*)

After the class has had a chance to browse through the poems in this section, choose which group you wish to join. Once in your groups you could ask yourselves:

Do you need to re-read the poems? Perhaps different members of the group could each read one of them.

Which poem did you like most? Can you say why?

Are there any poems, or parts of poems, which most of the group find difficult? Try to sort out any problems yourselves before asking your teacher to help.

Are there any lines, comparisons or phrases in the poems which particularly stay in your mind – perhaps because they create a mental picture, or contain an interesting idea, or simply because they sound unusual? Browse through the poems and talk about the passages which appeal to you.

Project

You may feel that you would like to be better acquainted with the writing of these five poets and use this selection simply as a starting-point for wider reading of their work by borrowing books from school and local libraries. A more demanding project would be to choose one of the five writers and not only read more widely but also build up a folder on the reading you have done, the life and background of the poet, what appeal you find in his work and perhaps include your own poems written in response to pieces by your chosen author. You may find that some of the poems we have printed are quite difficult but, with a bit of help from your teacher and some careful reading from you, there are ample opportunities here for a really worthwhile literary project of your own choosing.

It may be that, at the moment, you find such research on any of the five poets does not attract you. If so, you could follow up the work of any writer who does appeal to you. Jon Silkin, Stephen Spender, Douglas Dunn and Brian Jones are all fairly well represented in this anthology and may provide you with a starting-point for a project.

children's rhymes

In their book *The Lore and Language of Schoolchildren* (published by O.U.P.) Iona and Peter Opie gather together over 800 playground rhymes and chants along with a vast amount of fascinating information about slang, riddles, jokes, nicknames and so on. Some of the more common rhymes are given here to start you off remembering – if indeed you have forgotten.

What rhymes do you remember best?
– skipping rhymes, 'dipping' rhymes, singing games, rhyming riddles?
– rhymes about teachers, bigheads, cowards, crybabies, sneaks?
– rhymes about the end of term or ones said at a particular time of year, e.g. New Year, Christmas, Guy Fawkes night, 1st April?
-- adaptations of popular songs, hymns or carols?
– rhymes to tell you who you will marry or to prevent bad luck?

You will probably find many different ones, particularly if members of your class come from different parts of the country. Perhaps you could collect more from younger brothers and sisters and also from parents and grandparents. You could add to your store by listening to the youngest classes in your school when they play at break and lunchtimes. Perhaps you could seek permission to visit a local junior school and do some research for yourselves: with a cassette tape recorder you could make on-the-spot recordings. As you learn more about this subject you will find the Opies' book an invaluable guide.

Sam, Sam the dirty man,
Washed his face in a frying pan;
He combed his hair with a donkey's tail,
And scratched his belly with a big toe nail.   (general)

Oh my finger, oh my thumb,
Oh my belly, oh my bum.   (general)

Ladies and gentlemen
   Take my advice,
Pull down your pants
   And slide on the ice.   (general)

Isn't it funny, a rabbit's a bunny,
It has two ears, four legs, and a tummy.   (general)

Down in the valley where the grass grows green,
Sarah and her true love are always seen.
She blows, she blows, she blows so hard,
Run out, *Sarah*, while we choose your boy.
Does he love you? Yes-No-Yes-No etc. (until skipper falls over)
    (Skipping rhyme: Letchworth)

An Egg

A wee, wee hoose
Fou, fou o' meat,
Neither door nor window
To let you in to eat.
      (Riddle: Kirkcaldy)

A lighted candle

Little Nancy Netticoat
Wears a white petticoat
The longer she lives
The shorter she grows,
Little Nancy Netticoat.
      (Riddle: Shropshire)

I wet my finger,
I wipe it dry,
I cut my throat
If I tell a lie.
      (Swearing truth: Lydney)

Same to you with knobs on,
Cabbages with clogs on,
Elephants with slippers on,
And you with dirty knickers on.
      (Answering back: Lancashire)

Touch collar
Never swallow
Never get the fever,
Touch your nose
Touch your toes,
Never go in one of those.
      (To ward off ill luck on seeing
      an ambulance: Newcastle)

A duck in a pond,
A fish in a pool,
Whoever reads this
Is a big April fool.   (general)

While shepherds watched their turnip tops
    All boiling in the pot,
A lump of soot came rolling down
    And spoilt the bloomin' lot.   (general)

We three kings of Orient are
One in a taxi, one in a car,
One on a scooter blowing his hooter
Following yonder star.   (general)

Mary had a little lamb,
    She also had a bear;
I've often seen her little lamb
    But I've never seen her *bear*. (general)

In fourteen hundred and ninety-two
Columbus sailed the ocean blue;
He lost his yacht, the clumsy clot
That was a good one, was it not? (general)

Splishy splashy custard, dead dogs' eyes,
All mixed up with giblet pies,
Spread it on the butty nice and thick
Swallow it down with a bucket of sick.
      (School dinners: Manchester)

Sir is kind and sir is gentle,
Sir is strong and sir is mental.

… No more Latin, no more French
No more sitting on a hard board bench
No more English, no more stick,
No more flipping arithmetic …
      (End of term: general)

POEMS & PICTURES

Autumn Grove After Rain, by Wen Tien

Adrift in space,
The mountain's bare outline,
And a lower mountain's
Rocky waterfall – a white
Cleft on white mist –

With here a few
Slopes of pines,
And there a fall
Of mossy stones
That tumble soundlessly
Into a whiteness
That is either lake
Or sea or mist,
Or nothing –

On which a grove of trees
Floats away on flat rocks,
With a thatched summerhouse
And a tiny man
Fishing
From only
Half a bridge.

JAMES KIRKUP
(No. VII, *From* 'Seven
Pictures from China')

Landscape, by Ch'êng Sui

From a mountainside,
We look dizzily down
Through an ancient willow.

Across the bay
The peninsulas of rocks and trees
Fan the mist away
Into a poem on
A last inch of sky,
Indelible horizon.

In a narrow boat,
Curved and shallow as a leaf,
A lady and her boatman float
Upon the mist that hangs
Under and over their watery way.

She sits, with her white
Face lighting her black hair,
In the pale robe of ceremony.

The boatman in a pointed hat
Poles with dark hands
Their fragile craft
Towards a distant shore,
Where, set in a dry cliff among
Dark pines, a little house invents

A figure watching from an upper window
A dry leaf drifting on the misty bay.

JAMES KIRKUP
(No. V, *From* 'Seven Pictures from China')

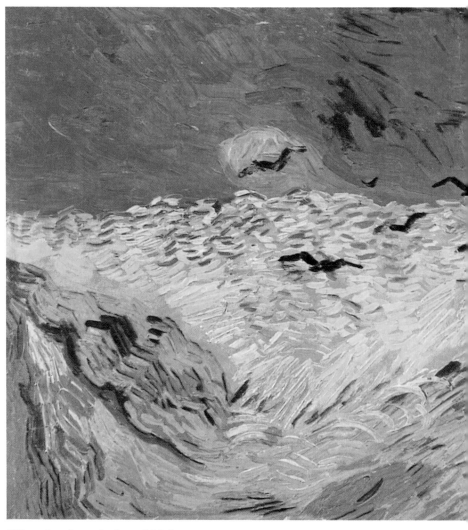

The Artist, Arles 1890

Yellow yellow
Watch the yellow always,
Fascinated, from the corner of your eye.
Its terrible intensity has sting
To bleach the brain, to take the skin
From off your inner eye. To drive you back
Against a buckled wall that echoes yellow, yellow
Pain. You cannot let it from your mind.   COLIN ROWBOTHAM

Van Gogh, Cornfield with Crows

The dirt-track uncoils and smears the gold,
Plunges tunnel-like and is lost.
Cornfields of Arles smash at the sky,

The crust of the earth buckles,
Slowly, painfully, like an animal.
No wind yet the sky whirls in hurricanes—
Blue, staining like blood
Gathering.
Midday meets with night in the sky.
Crows watch for the cracks.
The rocks sway under the roaring corn
As if hearing through a skin of sunstroke.
Drifting
Mad and blaring in the oils of his eyes,
The picture howls with fruitfulness.

JAMES O TAYLOR

101

In Breughel's Panorama

In Breughel's panorama of smoke and slaughter
Two people only are blind to the carrion army:
He, afloat in the sea of her blue satin
Skirts, sings in the direction
Of her bare shoulder, while she bends,
Fingering a leaflet of music, over him,
Both of them deaf to the fiddle in the hands
Of the death's-head shadowing their song.
These Flemish lovers flourish; not for long.

Yet desolation, stalled in paint, spares the little country
Foolish, delicate, in the lower right hand corner.

SYLVIA PLATH
(From *Two Views of a Cadaver Room*)

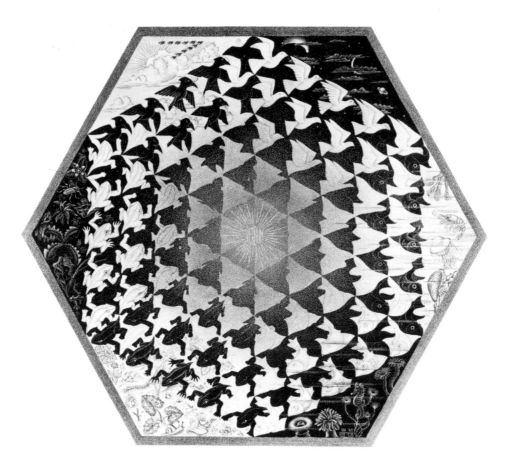

Look carefully at Escher's picture 'Verbum' above. What does it seem to show? Can you work out why he placed that particular Latin word at its centre?

If the picture suggests some interesting ideas to you then you may be able to use it as the basis for an original piece of writing along the lines suggested by other poets writing from pictures in this section.

Drama

Perhaps you could improvise from the picture with the class divided into groups working outwards from a centre and gradually gaining the forms of the different orders of creation represented – birds, reptiles, fish, sea-creatures, insects, snails (and any others you care to add). Music would help (e.g. the *2001 – A Space Odyssey* theme).

Poem-Cards (Materials: sheet of paper folded into card shape and size.)

Choose any picture from the book which appeals to you, trace it on to the front of your plain card and inside write your own poem in response to the picture. The two poems on pp. 100–101 were written by schoolboys about the picture above them. Possible variations are to make your own drawing or collage built up from cut-outs from magazines.

Group writing

Tell the story of Breughel's 'Triumph of Death' in verse (p. 102). Everyone adds a verse in turn. Plan it and develop the poem-story in whatever way seems best.

Mirror

I am silver and exact. I have no preconceptions.
Whatever I see I swallow immediately
Just as it is, unmisted by love or dislike.
I am not cruel, only truthful –
The eye of a little god, four-cornered.
Most of the time I meditate on the opposite wall.
It is pink, with speckles. I have looked at it so long
I think it is a part of my heart. But it flickers.
Faces and darkness separate us over and over.

Now I am a lake. A woman bends over me,
Searching my reaches for what she really is.
Then she turns to those liars, the candles or the moon.
I see her back, and reflect it faithfully.
She rewards me with tears and an agitation of hands.
I am important to her. She comes and goes.
Each morning it is her face that replaces the darkness.
In me she has drowned a young girl, and in me an old woman
Rises toward her day after day, like a terrible fish.

SYLVIA PLATH

A Strange Old Man

A strange old man
Stops me,
Looking out of my deep mirror.

HITOMARO
(*Trans. K Rexroth*)

Withered Reeds

Day after day
the withered reeds break off
and drift away.

RANKO
(Trans. H G Henderson)

The Door Knob

The room is curved in brass.
My fingers fill the room.

The closer that I come
to leaving the more huge.

the fingers till the room
is grown into a palm

whose one contraction will
obliterate the whole.

ROBIN SKELTON

Reflections – in rivers, pools and puddles, in mirrors, glass jars, polished floors and furniture, in spectacles and people's eyes – we are constantly surrounded by reflections. The ones which come to your mind most readily – apart, of course, from the flattering self-portrait you look at each morning – might be amusing, beautiful, or frightening. Most of us have come across the distortions produced by concave and convex mirrors or by the curved surfaces of a spoon, door knob or tap. And you may have noticed how strikingly beautiful effects can happen; the photograph by René Burri (pp. 106–7) is one of the most remarkable we have ever seen. It is simply a picture of reeds and grasses at the edge of a lake. Can you tell where the surface is? What is real and what is reflected?

Or again, you may have seen something in a reflection which perhaps momentarily frightened or disturbed you. What are your reactions to Escher's picture (p. 105) and Sylvia Plath's poem 'Mirror' (p. 104)?

There are many ways in which you could develop the theme of reflections. Here are some suggestions:

Drama
the mirror game
The class works in pairs, one person is 'real', the other the 'reflection'. Face each other and imagine a full-length mirror between you. Every movement and expression made by the 'real' person must be copied by the 'reflection'. It's difficult! Begin with simple, single movements and, slowly, make them more complex. Aim to be as exact as possible. Then change rôles.

Writing from pictures
There are three pictures in these pages, and another on p. 90, which might suggest a piece of writing to you. Or there may well be a photograph at home taken by you or your parents which you could use: reflections are a favourite subject with photographers. Whatever picture you use as a 'starter', try to describe the details precisely, concentrate on the thin line between reality and reflection and put down any thoughts that come to mind.

Shadows
Try to write a short piece entitled 'Shadows' – perhaps in haiku form like the poem on p. 104. Shadows can produce beautiful effects as they do in the photograph of the cat (p. 8); or the word may suggest more threatening and disturbing things to you.

Notebook
If it can be arranged officially, go down town or into a busy street with your notebook and jot down details of all the reflections you notice. (If this trip cannot be managed, you will find plenty of material around your own school building; or you could perhaps make notes on the way home from school). Try to find clear images to describe them. You may be struck by the distortion or oddness, by the colour or light; or you may be aware of the ghostliness of one thing superimposed upon another. Look particularly at your own reflection. These self-images may well suggest different things to you about yourself – different moods, characteristics, feelings. Let your mind wander over these images; you may be able to write a poem called, simply, 'Me'.

SHAPES

Watchwords

watch the words
watch words the
watchword is
watch words are   away.
sly as boots
ifyoutakeyoureyesoffthemforaminute

                    they're   up   and

                                         allover

                              the

                                    place

ROGER McGOUGH

110

Archives

```
generation upon
generation upon
generation upon
generation upon
generation upon
generation upon
generation upon
generation upon
generation upon
generation upon
generation upon
generation upon
generation upon
generation upon
generation upon
generation upon
generation upon
generation upon
g neration upon
g neration up  n
g nerat on up  n
g nerat  n up  n
g nerat  n  p  n
g  erat  n  p  n
g  era   n  p  n
g  era   n     n
g  er    n     n
g   r    n     n
g        n     n
g        n
g
```

EDWIN MORGAN

The Fan

Slowly, slowly
I unfold and Oh! what mysteries I behold:
with flowers and leaves my pattern
weaves and many creepers festoon
my trees. Beneath the amber wastes
of sky a loaded ox-cart trundles
by: the weary peasants wend
their way against the pale
of dying day. Gently
now I close again,
l i k e w a v e s
r e c e d i n g
w h e n c e
they
c
a
m
e.

MALCOLM TIMPERLEY

Easter Wings

Lord, who createdst man in wealth and store,
Though foolishly he lost the same,
Decaying more and more,
Till he became
Most poore:
With thee
O let me rise
As larks, harmoniously,
And sing this day thy victories:
Then shall the fall further the flight in me.

My tender age in sorrow did beginne:
And still with sicknesses and shame
Thou didst so punish sinne,
That I became
Most thinne.
With thee
Let me combine,
And feel this day thy victorie:
For, if I imp my wing on thine,
Affliction shall advance the flight in me.

GEORGE HERBERT

The Crosse-Tree

This Crosse-Tree here
Doth JESUS beare,
Who sweet'ned first,
The Death accurs't.
Here all things ready are, make hast, make hast away;
For, long this work wil be, & very short this Day.
Why then, go on to act: Here's wonders to be done,
Before the last least sand of Thy ninth houre be run;
Or e're dark Clouds do dull, or dead the Mid-dayes Sun.
Act when Thou wilt,
Bloud will be spilt;
Pure Balm, that shall
Bring Health to All.
Why then, Begin
To powre first in
Some Drops of Wine,
In stead of Brine,
To search the Wound,
So long unsound:
And, when that's done,
Let Oyle, next, run,
To cure the Sore
Sinne made before.
And O! Deare Christ,
E'en as Thou di'st,
Look down, and see
Us weepe for Thee.
And tho (Love knows)
Thy dreadfull Woes
Wee cannot ease;
Yet doe Thou please,
Who Mercie art,
T'accept each Heart,
That gladly would
Helpe, if it could.
Meane while, let mee,
Beneath this Tree,
This Honour have,
To make my grave.

ROBERT HERRICK

Revolver II

ALAN RIDDELL

Upon
His
Departure
Hence

Thus I
Passe by,
And die:
As One,
Unknown,
And gon:
I'm made
A shade,
And laid
I'th grave,
There have
My Cave.
Where tell
I dwell,
Farewell.

ROBERT HERRICK

here's a little mouse)and
what does he think about, i
wonder as over this
floor(quietly with

bright eyes)drifts(nobody
can tell because
Nobody knows, or why
jerks Here &, here,
gr(oo)ving the room's Silence)this like
a littlest
poem a
(with wee ears and see?

tail frisks)

       (gonE)

"mouse",
      We are not the same you and

i, since here's a little he
or is
it It
?   (or was something we saw in the mirror)?

therefore we'll kiss; for maybe
what was Disappeared
into ourselves
who   (look). ,startled

           e. e. cummings

Heart and Mirror

```
            IN
     ARE          THIS
   ONS              MIR
    I                ROR
  CT                  I
  LE                 AM
  REF                EN
  AS    Guillaume   CLOSED
        Apollinaire
  NOT                AL
  AND                IVE
  GELS               AND
    AN              REAL
     INE           AS
       MAG      YOU
          I
```

GUILLAUME APOLLINAIRE

116

Talking points

How do you react to these shape-poems? Fun? Irritating? Gimmicky? Thoughtful attempts at making a design with words? Substitutes for rhyme and metre?

Could any of these poems be printed normally without losing anything? Does the shape actually help you to understand the poem in each case?

Experiments

a)   Take some everyday object – your wristwatch, a pair of compasses, an elastic band, a ring, a coin, a piece of string, your hand itself – and try to write something brief but apt about the object you choose *in the shape of the object*. It might be helpful to sketch an outline of the object first.

b)   Now try starting with words and see what shapes they suggest or dictate. In each case think about the sound of the word and the associations it has for you in your mind's eye. Try these:

bee	oily	veins	rocks
branches	forked	blot	cloud

Some of these will not suggest any picture to you, let alone a particular shape, but try to work on one of them (or a word of your own) by drawing the outline it brings to mind and writing a description inside the outline.

Activities

1)   Try to write some shape poems.

One might use different line lengths to represent a silhouette of the subject of the poem on the page, as in 'Fan' (p. 112) and 'Easter Wings' (p. 116).

Another might be set out like Apollinaire's poems opposite, as though the letters were the actual lines of a drawing.

Or you may want to try a 'concrete' poem like 'Archives' (p. 111) or 'Revolver' (p. 114) where the visual lay-out is more important than the particular meaning of the words in the poem.

2)   Once you have made your two-dimensional poems try to turn them into three-dimensional ones. With some help from the Art Department, you can have a very enjoyable as well as surprisingly difficult period making 3-D shapes and structures from your shape poems. Some might be suitable as mobiles or classroom decoration.

3)   Trace the Leonardo picture (p. 115) and construct a shape poem, as Alan Riddell has done in 'Revolver' (p. 114), by arranging words, letters, ideas and comparisons to fit your tracing. Different words and ideas may be suggested by the cannon, the lines of fire, and the exploding shot.

SONGS

Little Boxes

Little boxes on the hillside, little boxes made of ticky-tacky,
Little boxes, little boxes, little boxes all the same;
There's a green one and a pink one and a blue one and a yellow one,
And they're all made out of ticky-tacky
And they all look just the same.

And the people in the houses all go to the university,
And they all get put in boxes, little boxes, all the same;
And there's doctors and there's lawyers and business executives,
And they're all made out of ticky-tacky
And they all look just the same.

And they all play on the golf course and drink their martini dry,
And they all have pretty children and the children go to school;
And the children go to summer camp and then to the university,
And they all get put in boxes
And they all come out the same.

And the boys go into business and marry and raise a family,
And they all get put in boxes, little boxes, all the same;
There's a green one and a pink one and a blue one and a yellow one,
And they're all made out of ticky-tacky
And they all look just the same.

M REYNOLDS
(Sung by Pete Seeger on CBS 68201)

Lucy in the Sky with Diamonds

Picture yourself in a boat on a river,
With tangerine trees and marmalade skies;
Somebody calls you, you answer quite slowly,
A girl with kaleidoscope eyes.
Cellophane flowers of yellow and green,
Towering over your head.
Look for the girl with the sun in her eyes,
And she's gone.
Lucy in the sky with diamonds.
Follow her down to a bridge by a fountain
Where rocking horse people eat marshmallow pies,
Everyone smiles as you drift past the flowers,
That grow so incredibly high.
Newspaper taxis appear on the shore,
Waiting to take you away.
Climb in the back with your head in the clouds,
And you're gone.
Lucy in the sky with diamonds.
Picture yourself on a train in a station,
With plasticine porters with looking glass ties,
Suddenly someone is there at the turnstile,
The girl with kaleidoscope eyes.

JOHN LENNON and PAUL McCARTNEY
(Sung by The Beatles on Sgt. Pepper PCS 7027)

She's Leaving Home

Wednesday morning at five o'clock as the day begins,
Silently closing her bedroom door,
Leaving the note that she hoped would say more,
She goes downstairs to the kitchen clutching her handkerchief;
Quietly turning the backdoor key,
Stepping outside she is free.
She (We gave her most of our lives)
is leaving (Sacrificed most of our lives)
home (We gave her everything money could buy).
She's leaving home after living alone
For so many years. Bye-bye.
Father snores as his wife gets into her dressing gown,
Picks up the letter that's lying there,
Standing alone at the top of the stairs
She breaks down and cries to her husband,
'Daddy, our baby's gone.
Why would she treat us so thoughtlessly?
How could she do this to me?'
She (We never thought of ourselves)
is leaving (Never a thought for ourselves)
home (We struggled hard all our lives to get by).
She's leaving home after living alone
For so many years. Bye-bye.
Friday morning at nine o'clock she is far away,
Waiting to keep the appointment she made,
Meeting a man from the motor trade.
She (What did we do that was wrong?)
is having (We didn't know it was wrong)
fun (Fun is the one thing that money can't buy).
Something inside that was always denied
For so many years. Bye-bye.
She's leaving home. Bye-bye.

JOHN LENNON and PAUL MCCARTNEY
(Sung by The Beatles on Sgt. Pepper – PCS 7027)

When I'm Sixty-Four

When I get older losing my hair,
Many years from now.
Will you still be sending me a Valentine,
Birthday greetings bottle of wine?
If I'd been out till quarter to three
Would you lock the door?
Will you still need me, will you still feed me,
When I'm sixty-four?
You'll be older too,
And if you say the word,
I could stay with you.
I could be handy, mending a fuse
When your lights have gone.
You can knit a sweater by the fireside,
Sunday morning go for a ride;
Doing the garden, digging the weeds,
Who could ask for more?
Will you still need me, will you still feed me,
When I'm sixty-four?
Every summer we can rent a cottage
In the Isle of Wight, if it's not too dear.
We shall scrimp and save;
Grandchildren on your knee,
Vera, Chuck and Dave.
Send me a postcard, drop me a line,
Stating point of view;
Indicate precisely what you mean to say
Yours sincerely, wasting away.
Give me your answer, fill in a form,
Mine for evermore;
Will you still need me, will you still feed me,
When I'm sixty-four?

JOHN LENNON and PAUL McCARTNEY
(Sung by the Beatles on Sgt. Pepper – PCS 7027)

Road Builders

'D'ye know I'd die if I didn't have this work. I couldn't do any
other work. I was often on these machines out in snow blizzards,
without anything over me, working up on the heights, and I still
prefer it. I still prefer the muck and the dirt and the grease
and everything to being inside a factory. Ah, I don't think I
could work in a factory.'

Jack Hamilton, bulldozer-driver on the M1, 1959.

The Driver's Song

Come all you gallant drivers, wherever you may be,
Whether you drive a Euclid or a fifty four R. B.;
Keep your hand upon the levers, Cut and fill a steady load,
And take it nice and steady when you're plowing up the road.

We've dug a hundred air fields, in the snow
and wind and rain,
Built atomic power stations, more dams
than I can name,
We've dug through rock and swampland,
moved mountains by the load,
Now we're going nice and steady, boys,
a-plowing up the road.

When your digging days are over and you've
loaded your last ton,
When your *cat* is broken up for scrap and
your ten R. B. won't run,
When you've had your last stamp on your
card and reached your last abode,
For a long time after there'll be people
travelling on your road.

Ewan MacColl

122

Come, Me Little Son

Come, me little son, and I will tell you what we'll do,
Undress yourself and get into bed and a tale I'll tell to you,
It's all about your daddy, he's a man you seldom see,
He's had to roam far away from home, away from you and me.
    But remember, lad, he's still your dad,
    though he's working far away
    In the cold and heat, eighty hours a week,
    on England's motorway.

When you fall and hurt yourself and get up feeling bad,
It isn't any use to go a running for your dad,
For the only time since you were born he's had to stay with you,
He was out of a job and we hadn't a bob, he was signing on the broo.*
    But remember, lad, he is still your dad,
    and he really earns his pay
    Working day and night upon the site
    of England's motorway.

To buy your shoes your daddy built a length of railway track.
He built a hydro-dam to buy the clothes upon your back,
This motor-highway buys the food but the wages soon are spent,
And though we have to live apart, it helps to pay the rent.
    But remember, lad, he is still your dad
    and he's toiling every day
    But there's food to be had and it's thanks to your dad
    on England's motorway.

Sure, we need your daddy here and sure it would be fine
To have him working nearer home and to see him all the time;
But beggars can't be choosers and we have to bear our load,
For we need the money your daddy earns a-working on the road.
    So remember, lad, he is still your dad
    and he'll soon be here to stay
    For a week or two with me and you
    when he's built the motorway.

Ewan MacColl

* labour exchange

The Fitter's Song

I am a roving rambler, a fitter to me trade;
I can fix you anything, a camshaft to a spade,
I can fix a dodgy gearbox or mend a broken tread,
De-coke a Leyland engine while I'm standing on me head.

So shift boys, shift, do the job and draw your pay.
When this job is finished, I'll be moving on me way,
I'll clean me tools and wrap 'em in a pair of oily jeans,
You'll always find me working where you find the big machines.

I've worked in far-off places since I left the *Coaly Tyne*,
I work among the heavies and I wear a roving sign,
I keep the tractors on the job a-turning up the soil,
I've followed my nose across the world by the smell of diesel oil.

So, shift, boys, shift, do the job and draw your pay,
When this job is finished I'll be moving on me way,
You'll find me where the tractors are, on roads and hydro-schemes,
Playing the lousy nursemaid to a pack of big machines.

EWAN MACCOLL

NOTE:
The last two songs can be found on the album
New Britain Gazette, FW 8732.
We would also recommend the following radio ballads
by Ewan MacColl, Charles Parker and Peggy Seeger:

The Big Hewer, dealing with the life of a miner–(DA 140).

The Fight Game, telling in song and interview the rise and
fall of a professional boxer–(DA 141).

Singing the Fishing, tracing the progress, through music and
song, of North Sea Fishing from 1899
to the present day–(DA 142).

The Travelling People, about gipsy life (DA 133).

Bridge over Troubled Water

When you're weary, feeling small,
When tears are in your eyes, I will dry them all;
I'm on your side. When times get rough
And friends just can't be found,
Like a bridge over troubled water
I will lay me down.
Like a bridge over troubled water
I will lay me down.

When you're down and out,
When you're on the street,
When evening falls so hard
I will comfort you.
I'll take your part.
When darkness comes
And pain is all around,
Like a bridge over troubled water
I will lay me down.
Like a bridge over troubled water
I will lay me down.

Sail on silvergirl,
Sail on by.
Your time has come to shine.
All your dreams are on their way.
See how they shine.
If you need a friend
I'm sailing right behind.
Like a bridge over troubled water
I will ease your mind.
Like a bridge over troubled water
I will ease your mind.

PAUL SIMON
(Sung by Simon and Garfunkel on CBS 63699)

Every time you listen to the lyric of a song, you are listening to a poem. Some songs have rather less in them than others and may seem to be little more than rhythmic repetitions of the same phrase or even vaguely animal grunts and howls – good for dancing and atmosphere but not very interesting when printed on the page.

Some singers seem to be more concerned with what they have to say, and on these pages we have printed a number of modern folk and pop lyrics that at different times have appealed to us or our classes. All very dated you might think. Fair enough: one of the great appeals of pop is that it changes continually, goes through fashions, is disposable – though we believe there are a number of very good pop lyrics that are certain to last. The less commercial modern folk songs of Ewan MacColl and Peggy Seeger may not be as well known to you but the best of them stand as poems in their own right.

Our first suggestion is that you should read these lyrics, talk about them as poems and, where possible, play the records on which they appear. Do any of them appeal more than others?

Now, if you were to compile your own collection of lyrics that seem to you to have something to say and to say it well, which ones would you include from the songs that have appeared over, say, the last eighteen months?

Do any recent pieces seem to you to be worthless? Can you say why?

Do your parents have a favourite song from when they were your age? Can you find the words? What do you think of the lyric and the music?

Looking & Seeing

Observation

*Now and then concentrating
on the very small,*

*focusing my attention
on a very small area*

*like this crack in sandstone
perpetually wet with seepage,*

*getting so close
to moss, liverwort and fern*

*it becomes a forest
with wild beasts in it,*

*birds in the branches
and crickets piping,*

*cicadas shrilling.
Someone seeing me*

*staring so fixedly
at nothing*

*might be excused
for thinking me vague, abstracted,*

*lost in introspection.
No! I am awake, absorbed,*

just looking in a different direction.

W HART-SMITH

Dandelion

Slugs nestle where the stem
Broken, bleeds milk.
The flower is eyeless: the sight is compelled
By small, coarse, sharp petals,
Like metal shreds. Formed,
They puncture, irregularly perforate
Their yellow, brutal glare.
And certainly want to
Devour the earth. With an ample movement
They are a foot high, as you look.
And coming back, they take hold
On pert domestic strains.
Others' lives are theirs. Between them
And domesticity,
Grass. They infest its weak land;
Fatten, hide slugs, infestate.
They look like plates; more closely
Like the first tryings, the machines, of nature
Riveted into her, successful.

JON SILKIN

Snowdrop

The blanched melted snows
Fill the plant's stem, a capillary
Of heightened moisture. Air weights
Round a white head hanging
Above granuled earth.
There, are three scarab-like petals,
Open, an insect's carapace
With a creature in these, poised.
It does not move. A white
Cylinder with two
Thin bands of green, broken
Away where that part finishes.
There is no more.
The sun's heat reaches the flower
Of the snowdrop.

JON SILKIN

Meditation at Oyster River *Part 1*

Over the low, barnacled, elephant-colored rocks,
Come the first tide-ripples, moving, almost without sound, toward me,
Running along the narrow furrows of the shore, the rows of dead clam shells;
Then a runnel behind me, creeping closer,
Alive with tiny striped fish, and young crabs climbing in and out of the water.

No sound from the bay. No violence.
Even the gulls quiet on the far rocks,
Silent, in the deepening light,
Their cat-mewing over,
Their child-whimpering.

At last one long undulant ripple,
Blue-black from where I am sitting,
Makes almost a wave over a barrier of small stones,
Slapping lightly against a sunken log.
I dabble my toes in the brackish foam sliding forward,
Then retire to a rock higher up on the cliff-side.
The wind slackens, light as a moth fanning a stone:
A twilight wind, light as a child's breath
Turning not a leaf, not a ripple.
The dew revives on the beach-grass;
The salt-soaked wood of a fire crackles;
A fish raven turns on its perch (a dead tree in the rivermouth),
Its wings catching a last glint of the reflected sunlight.

THEODORE ROETHKE

Relic

I found this jawbone at the sea's edge:
There, crabs, dogfish, broken by the breakers or tossed
To flap for half an hour and turn to a crust
Continue the beginning. The deeps are cold:
In that darkness camaraderie does not hold:
Nothing touches but, clutching, devours. And the jaws,
Before they are satisfied or their stretched purpose
Slacken, go down jaws; go gnawn bare. Jaws
Eat and are finished and the jawbone comes to the beach:
This is the sea's achievement; with shells,
Vertebrae, claws, carapaces, skulls.

Time in the sea eats its tail, thrives, casts these
Indigestibles, the spars of purposes
That failed far from the surface. None grow rich
In the sea. This curved jawbone did not laugh
But gripped, gripped and is now a cenotaph.

TED HUGHES

Perfect

On The Western Seaboard of South Uist

*Los muertos abren los ojos a los que viven**

I found a pigeon's skull on the machair†,
All the bones pure white and dry, and chalky,
But perfect,
Without a crack or a flaw anywhere.

At the back, rising out of the beak,
Were domes like bubbles of thin bone,
Almost transparent, where the brain had been
That fixed the tilt of the wings.

Words by GLYN JONES,
arranged as a poem by
HUGH MACDIARMID

*the dead open the eyes of the living
†low-lying sandy beach or marsh

The Chalk Blue Butterfly

The Chalk Blue (clinging to
A harebell stem, where it loops
Its curving wirefine neck
From which there hangs the flowerbell
Shaken by the wind that shakes
Too, the butterfly) –
Opens now, now shuts, its wings,
Opening, shutting, on a hinge
Sprung at touch of sun or shadow.
   Open, the sunned wings mirror
Minute, double, all the sky.
   Shut, the ghostly underwing
Is cloud-opaque, bordered by
Copper spots embossed
By a pigmy hammering.

   I look and look, as though my eyes
Could hold the Chalk Blue in a vice,
Waiting for some other witness
—That child's blue gaze, miraculous.
But today I am alone.

STEPHEN SPENDER

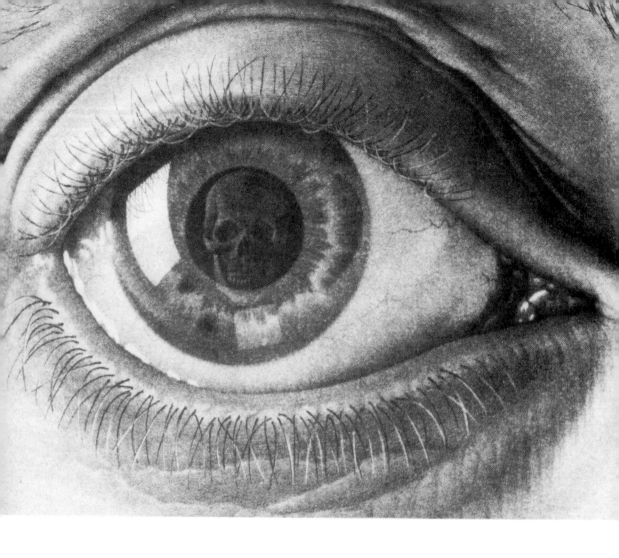

The writers and artists in this section all concentrate on looking very closely at small details and in so doing make us aware that these can be important. We no longer just *look*: we *see*, as well. In this workshop we suggest that you should explore the textures, colours and close details of the natural world in much the same way.

1) Jon Silkin writes about the dandelion and the snowdrop and gives us close-up word-pictures of these. Try to do the same for some other plant or flower. If at all possible work with the subject before you. Look carefully at every detail and jot down ideas in rough first. Use all your senses where possible.

2) 'Relic' and 'Perfect' (p. 130) both use the bones of dead creatures as their starting-point. If you can, look carefully at bones and skulls in your Biology laboratory or – better still – borrow them and handle them in class, then you may be able to write on a similar theme. Fossils too are a good starting-point; so are shells. A visit to your local museum may also provide you with the chance to look at things in detail.

3)　M. C. Escher sees a skull in the pupil of his own eye in the picture opposite. Instead of using your eyes as windows to peer from, look inwards. What images do you imagine there? Try to draw them and write about them.

Bringing objects into the classroom

From home you may have:
　shells, pebbles, driftwood, pressed flowers …

From science laboratories:
　stick insects, locusts, magnets and iron filings, prisms, crystals, magnifying glass …

Easily obtainable from outside:
　leaves, twigs, bark, flowers, stones, moss …

With a little care and organisation each of you could provide yourself with an object of your own choosing. Aim to record the details of its shape, colours, textures etc. but let your thoughts and feelings wander: a small shell can open up a whole landscape if you let it.

Drama

For most of us, sight dominates the five senses. The drama exercise of 'walking blind', with which you may already be familiar, makes you rely on touch and hearing.

　In a large empty space, split into pairs, one 'sighted' and the other 'blind'. The 'sighted' partner turns the 'blind' one around to confuse his sense of direction and then leads him carefully, but at varying speeds, around the room. If drama blocks can be used as obstacles, then he may lead his partner over these, *always with the greatest care*. The 'sighted' partners move to the perimeter of the room, taking their partners with them, and move at steadily increasing speed in a large circle. There are obviously many similar exercises, e.g. trying to get out of the room, blind, in an emergency. After these exercises compare notes. What was it like to move quickly without the benefit of sight? How important were sounds? How important was touch? What sort of details did you notice? What effect did 'blindness' have on the way you moved? Ask your partners about these things. You might feel able to write an imaginative account of blindness concentrating particularly on details.

MASKS

Poem to be Cast
in Bronze

A mask and
not a mask.
We have no face

only the space
behind the mask,
the mask

upon the mask
upon the
mask upon –

is it bone
or the dark
of a long-dead star?

ROBIN SKELTON

The Mask of Evil

On my wall hangs a Japanese carving,
The mask of an evil demon, decorated with gold lacquer.
Sympathetically I observe
The swollen veins of the forehead, indicating
What a strain it is to be evil.

BERTOLT BRECHT

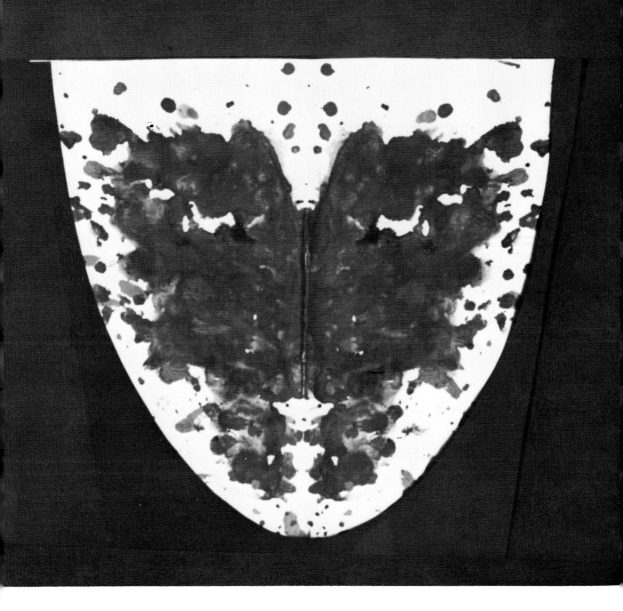

1)   Make a mask that will fit you and decorate it in any way you like. When your mask is finished, put it on and talk to a partner in the way you feel fits the character of the mask.

Write about what you felt and noticed when your partner wore his or her mask. Was it sad, funny or frightening? How far was the person able to express his feelings? Did it make the person stronger or weaker? What else did you notice or feel?

2)   How do you think the inkblot mask on this page was made? Try to make one yourself at the top of a sheet of paper and underneath it write about the ideas it suggests.

Acknowledgements

Thanks are due to the authors (or their executors), their representatives and publishers mentioned in the following list for their kind permission to reproduce copyright material:

Jon Silkin: 'Caring for Animals', 'Death of a Bird' and 'Snowdrop' from *Poems New and Selected*; 'Dandelion' from *Nature With Man* Chatto & Windus Ltd

Carl Sandburg: 'Wilderness' from *Cornhuskers*; 'Who do you think you are?' from *The People, Yes* Harcourt Brace Jovanovich Inc.

Douglas Livingstone: 'The King' from *Sjambok and Other Poems from Africa* © Oxford University Press 1964

Alan Brownjohn: 'Cat' and 'Parrot' from *Brownjohn's Beasts*; 'The Rabbit' from *The Railings* the Digby Press and Macmillan, London and Basingstoke

Seamus Heaney: 'The Early Purges', 'Death of a Naturalist', 'Blackberry Picking', 'Digging' and 'The Barn' from *Death of a Naturalist*; 'The Forge' from *Door Into the Dark*; 'Limbo' from *Wintering Out* Faber & Faber Ltd

May Swenson: 'The Secret in the Cat' from *Half Sun Half Sleep* by May Swenson, Copyright 1967 by May Swenson and Charles Cribner's Sons New York, reprinted by permission of the author

Colin Rowbotham for 'Dissection'; Malcolm Timperley for 'The Fan' and Graham Walley for 'Death of God' from *Ulula* The Manchester Grammar School

Theodore Roethke: 'Meadow Mouse', 'The Lizard' and 'Meditation at Oyster River' from *The Collected Poems* Faber & Faber Ltd. Copyright © 1963, 1961, 1960 by Beatrice Roethke, Administratrix of the Estate of Theodore Roethke from the book *Collected Poems of Theodore Roethke*. Reprinted by permission of Doubleday Company Inc.

John Haines: 'If the Owl Calls Again' and 'And When the Green Man Comes' from *Winter News* copyright © 1961, 1962, (by John Haines) Wesleyan University Press

Michael Benedikt: 'Thoughts' from *The Body* copyright © 1968 by Michael Benedikt, Wesleyan University Press

George Macbeth: 'Owl' by permission of the author

Walter de la Mare: 'Winter' and 'A Robin' by permission of The Literary Trustees of Walter de la Mare and The Society of Authors as their representative

Stevie Smith: 'Best Beast at the Fatstock Show' from *Frog Prince and Other Poems* Longman

Sylvia Plath: 'Mirror' from *Crossing the Water*; 'In Breughel's Panorama', 'Mushrooms', 'A Winter Ship' and 'Metaphors' from *The Colossus*; 'Balloons', 'The Arrival of the Bee Box', 'Morning Song' and 'You're' from *Ariel* by courtesy of Miss Olwyn Hughes

Denise Levertov: 'To the Snake' from *Eyes at the Back of Our Heads*. Copyright © 1958 by Denise Levertov Goodman. Reprinted by permission of New Directions Publishing Corporation, New York and Laurence Pollinger Ltd and 'The Disclosure' from *O Taste and See*. Copyright © 1964 by Denise Levertov Goodman. Reprinted by permission of New Directions Publishing Corporation, New York

Emily Dickinson: 'Snake' reprinted by permission of the publishers and the Trustees of Amherst College from Thomas H Johnson, Editor *The Poems of Emily Dickinson*, Cambridge Mass: The Belknap Press of Harvard University Press, Copyright, 1951, 1955, by the President and Fellows of Harvard College

James Kirkup: 'Landscape' and 'Autumn Grove After Rain' by permission of the author and 'Baby's Drinking Song' from *White Shadows Black Shadows* J M Dent & Sons Ltd

Tony Connor: 'Child Half Asleep' from *Kon In Springtime* © Oxford University Press 1968

R S Thomas 'Children's Song' from *Song at the Year's Turning* Granada Publishing Ltd

Robert Graves: 'Warning to Children' from *Collected Poems 1965* A P Watt & Son, by permission of Robert Graves

Stephen Spender: 'To My Daughter' and 'My Parents Kept Me from Children Who Were Rough' from *Collected Poems 1928–1953*; 'Fifteen Line Sonnet in Four Parts' and 'The Chalk Blue Butterfly' from *The Generous Days* Faber & Faber Ltd

Elaine Feinstein: 'At Seven a Son'; David Harsent: 'Rag Doll to the Heedless Child'; Jeremy Hooker: 'Winter Moon' from *Poetry Introduction 1* Faber & Faber Ltd, (by permission of the authors)

Brian Jones: 'Thaw', 'How to Catch Tiddlers' and 'Visiting Miss Emily' from *Poems and a Family Album* London Magazine Editions

John Haines: 'The Cauliflower', 'In Nature' and 'Dream of a Cardboard Lover' from *The Stone Harp* Andre Deutsch Ltd

Robin Skelton: 'The Door Knob' and 'Poem to be Cast in Bronze' from *The Hunting Dark* Andre Deutsch Ltd

William Meredith: 'Fledglings' from *Earth Walk: New and Selected Poems* Alfred A Knopff Inc.

Langston Hughes: 'The Ballad of the Landlord' from *Montage of a Dream Deferred* Harold Ober Associates; 'Dream Variation' from *Selected Poems* Alfred A Knopff Inc.

Andrey Voznesensky: 'First Ice', translated by George Reavey, reprinted with George Reavey's permission

Douglas Dunn: 'Love Poem', 'On Roofs of Terry Street' and 'From the Night Window' from *Terry Street* Faber & Faber Ltd

The Reverend F Pratt Green: 'The Old Couple', first published in *The Listener* August 1964, reprinted by permission of the author

D H Lawrence: 'Old People' from *The Complete Poems of D H Lawrence* Laurence Pollinger Ltd and the Estate of the late Mrs Frieda Lawrence

G M Hopkins: 'Clouds' from *Diaries and Journals by G M Hopkins* Oxford University Press

Norman MacCaig: 'Summer Waterfall, Glendale' from *Measures*; 'Hotel Room, 12th Floor' from *Rings on a Tree*; 'Moorings' from *A Round of Applause* Chatto & Windus Ltd

George MacKay Brown: 'Weather Bestiary' from *The Year of the Whale* Chatto & Windus Ltd

Elizabeth Bishop: 'At the Fishouses' from *Poems*

hatto and Windus Ltd, A M Heath & Company (Authors' Agents) and Farrar Strauss & Giroux Inc.

Anthony Thwaite: 'A Haiku Yearbook' from *Inscriptions* Oxford University Press

Wes Magee: 'Sunday Morning' from *Poetry Introduction* Faber & Faber Ltd, by permission of the author

Philip Larkin: 'To the Sea' from *High Windows* Faber & Faber Ltd

Richard Ryan: 'A Heap of Stones' from *Poetry Introduction 2* Faber & Faber Ltd, first published by Dolmen Press, Dublin, reprinted by permission of the author

Roger McGough: 'Watchwords' and 'The Hippopotamusman' from *Watchwords* by Roger McGough, Jonathan Cape Ltd

Kenneth Rexroth: 'I return to the Place Where I was Born' by T'ao Yuan Ming from *Love and the Turning Year* Copyright © 1970 by Kenneth Rexroth reprinted by permission of New Directions Publishing Corporation, New York; 'A Strange Old Man' by Hitomaro from *One Hundred Poems from the Japanese*. All Rights Reserved, reprinted by permission of New Directions Publishing Corporation, New York, and Laurence Pollinger Ltd

Philip Hobsbaum: 'The Place's Fault' from *The Place's Fault and Other Poems* Macmillan, London and Basingstoke

Ted Hughes: 'Relic' and 'Snowdrop' from *Lupercal*; 'Examination at the Womb-Door', 'Crow's Song of Himself' and 'King of Carrion' from *Crow*; 'The Jaguar' from *The Hawk in the Rain*; 'The Howling of Wolves' from *Wodwo*; extract from 'Capturing Animals' from *Poetry in the Making* reprinted by permission of Faber & Faber Ltd

Robert Frost: 'The Road Not Taken', 'Lodged', 'Nothing Gold can Stay', 'Design', 'The Runaway', 'Spring Pools', 'Out, out–', and 'At Woodwards Gardens' from *The Poetry of Robert Frost* edited by Edward Connery Lathem, reproduced by permission of Jonathan Cape Ltd and the Estate of Robert Frost, Copyright 1916, 1923, 1928, 1969 by Holt Rinehart and Winston Inc. Copyright 1936, 1944, 1951, 1956 by Robert Frost. Copyright 1964 by Lesley Frost Ballantine. Reprinted by permission of Holt, Rinehart & Winston Inc. Publishers New York

Brian Patten: 'Little Johnny's Confession', 'Little Johnny's Final Letter', 'Mr Jones Takes Over', 'The Projectionist's Nightmare', 'Bombscare' and 'A Small Dragon' from *Notes to the Hurrying Man* George Allen & Unwin Ltd

Ranko: 'The Withered Reeds' from *An Introduction to Haiku* by Harold G Henderson. Copyright © 1958 by Harold G Henderson. Reprinted by permission of Doubleday & Company Inc.

Edwin Morgan: 'Archives' from *The Second Life* Edinburgh University Press

Bertolt Brecht: 'The Mask of Evil' © Copyright by Stefan S Brecht 1964, Eyre Methuen Ltd

W Hart Smith: 'Observation' from *The Unceasing Ground* Angus & Robertson (UK) Ltd

Guillaume Apollinaire: 'Heart' and 'Mirror' from *Calligrammes* © Editions Gallimard 1925

e. e. cummings: 'here's a little mouse) and' from *Complete Poems Volume 1* Granada Publishing Ltd and Harcourt Brace Jovanovich Inc.

Hugh MacDiarmid, Glyn Jones: 'Perfect' words by Glyn Jones, arranged as a poem by Hugh MacDiarmid

Malvina Reynolds: the lyrics of 'Little Boxes' TRO Essex Music Ltd

Ewan MacColl: the lyrics of 'The Driver's Song', 'Come, me little Son' and 'The Fitter's Song' Harmony Music Ltd

John Lennon and Paul McCartney: 'Lucy in the Sky with Diamonds', 'She's Leaving Home' and 'When I'm 64' lyrics used by permission of Northern Songs Ltd, 12 Bruton St London © 1967

Paul Simon: 'Bridge over Troubled Water' © 1970 by Paul Simon. Controlled for the British Isles by Pattern Music Ltd, 5 Denmark St London. Reproduced with Permission

The Authors wish to thank the following for permission to reproduce photographs:

Cover and title-page photograph by Peter Keen

The William Blake Trust and *the Trianon Press* 'The Tyger' William Blake

Albertina Museum, Vienna 'The Lion', 'The Dead Bird', 'The Rhinoceros' Dürer

Fitzwilliam Museum, Cambridge: 'Kittens' J B Oudry

Linwu Kai-Chou 'Cat'; *Zdeněk Holoček* 'Wild Rabbit' from Photography Year Book 1971

A Lauw 'Owl'

The John Hillelson Agency Ltd 'Bird and Tap', 'Mother and Baby' Elliott Erwitt; 'Cattle', 'City Scene, USA', 'Lake Reflections' René Burri; 'Children Bathing in Hydrant' Leonard Freed; 'Lotus Pool' Werner Bischof

Bill Brandt 'Caligo', 'Avebury Stone Circle', 'Policeman, Bermondsey'

Henry Moore 'Helmet Head No 2', 'Family Group' from the collection of Miss Mary Moore

Chung-Chuan Huang 'Two Boys Jump from the Bank of a River'

Collection: Escher Foundation, Haags Gemeentemuseum, The Hague 'Metamorphose II' 'Fluorescent Sea', 'Puddle', 'Three Worlds', 'Eye', 'Verbum' M C Escher

Tate Gallery 'They're Biting', Paul Klee

Munch-Museet, Oslo 'The Kiss', Edvard Munch

The British Museum 'Memento Mei', Dürer; 'Autumn Grove After Rain' Wen Tien; 'Landscape' Cheng Sui

The Trustees, The National Gallery, London 'A Winter Scene with Skaters' Avercamp

Royal Academy of Arts, London 'Study of Clouds and Trees (Sept 1821)' John Constable

The Royal Library, Windsor 'The Unborn Child', Leonardo da Vinci

Faber & Faber Ltd Sylvia Plath

Fay Goodwin Ted Hughes, Seamus Heaney, by courtesy of Faber & Faber Ltd

Jonathan Cape Ltd Robert Frost

Leonard Baskin 'Crow' by courtesy of Faber & Faber Ltd

George Allen & Unwin Ltd Brian Patten

Gustave Doré 'The Land of Ice' from 'Rime of the Ancient Mariner' by S Coleridge, published by *Dover Publications Inc, New York*

The Louvre Gallery 'Monkeys' Pisanello

Kunsthistoriches Museum, Vienna 'Children's Games' Pieter Breughel

M L Madsen 'Volkswagen Reflections'

The Prado Museum, Madrid 'The Triumph of Death' Pieter Breughel

Professor J Cohen and *G Allen & Unwin Ltd* 'Diabolic Face produced by a child's ink blots'

R Canessa 'Electronic City'

Biblioteca Ambrosiana, Milan 'Bombardment by Exploding Shot' Leonardo da Vinci

M Carrebye from the Beatles film "A fool on the Hill"

Stedelijk Museum, Amsterdam 'Landscape: Cornfield with Crows' Van Gogh

'To the Snake' typesetting by Apex Ltd, 8 Vine Hill, London

Design by Lynda Sullivan

ISBN 0 340 16201 5

First published 1975
Thirteenth impression 1993

Printed in Great Britain for
Hodder and Stoughton Educational,
a division of Hodder and Stoughton Ltd,
Mill Road, Dunton Green, Sevenoaks, Kent,
by Butler & Tanner Ltd,
Frome and London